WBI DEVELOPMENT STUDIES

Accounting for Poverty in Infrastructure Reform

Learning from Latin America's Experience

Antonio Estache
Vivien Foster
Quentin Wodon

A joint publication of the World Bank Institute,
the World Bank's Latin America and Caribbean
Regional Studies Program, the Latin America and Caribbean
Finance, Private Sector, and Infrastructure Department,
and the Latin America and Caribbean Poverty Reduction
and Economic Management Department

The World Bank
Washington, D.C.

The World Bank Institute was established by the World Bank in 1955 to train officials concerned with development planning, policymaking, investment analysis, and project implementation in member developing countries. At present the substance of WBI's work emphasizes macroeconomic and sectoral policy analysis. Through a variety of courses, seminars, workshops, and other learning activities, most of which are given overseas in cooperation with local institutions, WBI seeks to sharpen analytical skills used in policy analysis and to broaden understanding of the experience of individual countries with economic and social development. Although WBI's publications are designed to support its training activities, many are of interest to a much broader audience.

Antonio Estache is a lead economist in the Governance, Regulation, and Finance Division of the World Bank Institute. Vivien Foster is an economist in the World Bank's Latin America and Caribbean Region, Finance, Private Sector, and Infrastructure Department. Quentin Wodon is a senior economist in the World Bank's Latin America and Caribbean Region's Poverty Sector Group.

Library of Congress Cataloging-in-Publication Data

Estache, Antonio.
    Accounting for poverty in infrastructure reform : learning from Latin America's
experience / Antonio Estache, Vivien Foster, Quentin Wodon.
      p. cm.—(WBI development studies)
    Includes bibliographical references.
    ISBN 0-8213-5039-0
    1. Public utilities—Latin America. 2. Poverty—Latin America. 3. Privatization—Latin
America. I. Foster, Vivien. II. Wodon, Quentin. III. Title. IV. Series.

HD2768.L292 E88 2001
363'.098—dc21

    2001046928

Contents

Foreword

This book explores the connections between infrastructure reform and poverty alleviation in Latin America based on a detailed analysis of the effects of a decade of reforms. It demonstrates that because the access to, and affordability of, basic services is still a major problem, infrastructure investment will be a core component of poverty alleviation programs in the region. The book shows that although affordability of service tariffs is often an issue, in many instances, access is a much more important concern in meeting the infrastructure needs of the poor. Thus, infrastructure provision is a key poverty-reduction tool.

The book's main goal is to provide practical guidelines and methods to help policymakers, reformers, and regulators develop diagnostics to assess infrastructure needs and to ensure that strategies to address them are as cost effective as possible. Special emphasis is placed on data collection and explanations of some of the quantitative methodologies that can serve as inputs to the studies needed to ensure that the poor are accounted for under any form of infrastructure provision.

This volume is the result of a combination of research, policy analysis, and capacity-building efforts, and reflects the contributions of a wide range of policymakers, academics, and user representatives consulted during courses and seminars organized by the World Bank Institute in Latin America, Europe, and Africa where it was used to fuel the debate on the effects of infrastructure reform on the poor.

We hope that *Accounting for Poverty in Infrastructure Reform* will be useful to policymakers throughout the developing world and will continue to serve as an instrument of dialogue among all the actors involved in infrastructure provision and reform.

Frannie A. Léautier
Vice President
World Bank Institute

Danny M. Leipziger
Director
Finance, Private Sector
   and Infrastructure Department
Latin America Region, World Bank

Acknowledgments

This report was funded by a research grant from the Regional Studies Program, Office of the Chief Economist (Guillermo Perry) for the Latin America and Caribbean Region, World Bank. Partial funding was also received from the World Bank Institute, from joint work with the Bolivia, Guatemala, and Honduras poverty assessments, and from the ESMAP project on low income energy assistance in Latin America.

This report is supported by a series of background papers and notes prepared by, in addition to the lead authors, Mohamed Ihsan Ajwad, Bernadette Ryan, Corinne Siaens, and Jean-Philippe Tre, all of whom were consultants in the World Bank's Latin America Region, Poverty Group, at the time of writing. References to these background papers and notes are made throughout the text. Anna Wellenstein from the Urban Development Group of the World Bank's Latin America Region also provided valuable input.

Various sections of the report were presented and discussed at seminars in Argentina, Benin, Brazil, Côte d'Ivoire, Ethiopia, Finland, France, Ghana, Guinea, Mauritania, Nigeria, Senegal, Spain, Tanzania, Togo, Uganda, and Uruguay. Special thanks are due to technical reviewers Phil Gray and Catherine Waddams for advice during the preparation of this book, and to the advisory committee for this research project: Danny Leipziger, Nora Lustig, and Michael Walton. Norman Hicks, Ernesto May, Michael Kerf, Luis Serven, and Lourdes Trujillo also provided valuable guidance and suggestions. We are also indebted to many colleagues at the World Bank and in privatization and regulatory commissions throughout Latin America for their kindness in sharing their experience with us.

1

Introduction

This book explores conceptually and empirically the connections between infrastructure reform and poverty in Latin American. After a brief historical review of the Latin American infrastructure reform experience and its impact on the poor, it covers the various ways poverty concerns can be addressed in the context of increased private sector participation in infrastructure. It shows why infrastructure investment is likely to continue to be a core component of many poverty alleviation programs. It also emphasizes why and how, in most countries, infrastructure reform aimed at promoting private financing of investment must be carefully designed to consider poverty concerns. The book's ultimate goal, however, is to provide practical guidelines and options to ensure that the strong needs for additional infrastructure investments are met and that the strategies to address the needs of the poor are as cost-effective as possible. The emphasis throughout is on providing practical guidelines and options for the future, grounded in rigorous analytical support.

Chapter 2 overviews the transmission mechanisms through which infrastructure reform may affect the poor, at the macro- and microeconomic levels. As the World Bank and others are currently studying the macroeconomic impact of the reforms, this study focuses on microeconomic issues related to access to infrastructure services for the poor and the affordability of these services (for more information about macroeconomic linkages see www.wider.unu.edu).

Chapter 3 reviews the trends in access to infrastructure services in Latin America, specifically, electricity, water, and telephone services, and examines whether the poor are benefiting from overall increases in connections. The chapter then discusses in detail the options available to policymakers for promoting better access.

Chapter 4 discusses the options available to policymakers for ensuring service affordability.

Chapter 5 discusses the relationships between access and affordability, the impact of both on poverty, and the establishment of priorities. Two questions receive specific attention. First, within a given sector, should policymakers emphasize subsidies for new connections or consumption subsidies among those already benefiting from existing connections? Second, are policies in some sectors more important or appropriate for poverty reduction than in other sectors?

Much of what is discussed in this book is intended to help policymakers think through the tradeoffs between efficiency, equity, and the fiscal consequences of the various options (see Crampes and Estache 1998 or Estache and Quesada 2001 for a more conceptual approach). The study is designed to be relevant to regulators who must focus on access and tariff design issues and try to identify solutions that can improve both efficiency and equity. It includes a set of instruments intended to provide analytical support to decisions in setting priorities, recognizing that, as in most areas touching on regulation, the tradeoffs between efficiency, equity, and fiscal costs ultimately require political decisions that are beyond the scope of this study. This study builds on more general work about the linkages between poverty and the infrastructure sectors that has been supported by the World Bank in the context of the highly indebted poor countries initiative (for further details refer to the *Poverty Reduction Strategy Papers Sourcebook* at www.worldbank.org/poverty/strategies/sourcons.htm).

Background

Until the 1980s, state-owned enterprises with local or national service monopolies provided utility services in most countries in Latin America. During the 1990s fiscal constraints and growing dissatisfaction with the poor efficiency, quality, and coverage of service provided by many state-owned utilities generated the necessary political momentum for reform. The number of countries in Latin America that have pursued or are pursuing utility sector liberalization policies and are trying to rely on increased private sector participation grew dramatically in the last decade. These reforms generated total investments (private plus linked government) in Latin America of $290 billion between 1990 and 1999, which represents almost half of all private investment in the infrastructure sector in developing countries. (All dollar amounts are U.S. dollars.) While the reforms were initially concentrated in South America (led by Argentina, Bolivia, and Chile), Central America and the Caribbean are now in their own privatization phase.

Table 1.1. *Overview of Infrastructure Reforms in Latin America and the Caribbean, 1990s*

Country	Management contracts	Concessions	BOT contracts	Divestiture or sales
Argentina	n.a.	W&S (1991–2000) E (Gas) (1992–98)	E (1992–99)	T (1990) E (1992–98)
Bolivia	n.a.	W&S (1997–99)	E (1999)	T (1995) E (1995–97)
Brazil	W&S (1997–98)	W&S (1995–98) E (1998–2000)	E (1984–99) W&S (1995–98)	T (1998) E (1998–99)
Chile	n.a.	n.a.	E (1990–97)	T (1988–90) E (1989–98) W&S (1999)
Colombia	W&S (1995–97)	n.a.	E (1993–99) W&S (1994)	E (1996–98)
Dominican Republic	n.a.	n.a.	E (1989–96)	E (1998–99)
El Salvador	n.a.	n.a.	E (1998)	T (1998) E (1998)
Guatemala	n.a.	n.a.	E (1998)	T (1998) E (1998)
Mexico	W&S (1996–99)	W&S (1997–99)	E (1995–99)	T (1989) E (1998–99)
Peru	n.a.	n.a.	E (1997–99)	T (1993) E (1994–98)
Uruguay	n.a.	W&S (1997–2000)	T (1995–97)	n.a.
Venezuela	W&S (1997)	n.a.	n.a.	T (1991)

n.a. Not applicable.
BOT Build-operate-transfer.
E Energy.
T Telecommunications.
W&S Water and sewerage.
Source: Authors.

While casual observers continue to associate infrastructure reforms with privatization, implying a sale of assets, the reality is subtler. Table 1.1 shows the distribution across sectors and types of contracts in a large sample of Latin American countries during the last decade. Contracts for private sector participation can be classified into four main categories: management contracts, concessions, BOT (build-operate-transfer) contracts, and divestiture or sales. In water and sanitation, management contracts and concessions are the norm. BOT contracts have been considered for major new constructions such as waste and water treatment plants, but few deals have actually taken place. In energy and telecommunications, concessions and full divestiture are standard. In many countries in isolated regions that are too distant from the main networks, private operators have long been the main providers and have remained so after the reform. Most of what is discussed in this book applies to all forms of private sector participation adopted in infrastructure sector reform and can be addressed in conjunction with any of the contract options found in Latin America. We will thus use a broad definition of private sector participation to address the nexus between poverty and private provision of infrastructure, and only distinguish between types of contracts when necessary.

Investment and Reform Needs

While the achievements are considerable, the work that remains to be done is still challenging. According to Fay (2000), the annual investments needed for 2000–05 should amount to about $57 billion, equivalent to 2.6 percent of Latin America's gross domestic product (GDP). Maintenance is estimated at $35 billion per year. Rehabilitation needs cannot be estimated given the absence of systematic data across sectors on the current state of infrastructure. All this represents a significant potential business for private investors, but this business is unlikely to focus on the needs of the poor unless explicit policy effort is made with that purpose in mind.

Reforms offer the potential to improve services to the poor in two main areas: access and affordability. Improvements in access refers to users' ability to obtain new connections. Affordability refers to whether poor households are able to pay the charges for using the service once they have it. Reforms can help improve both access and affordability. Access may be improved through private financing that makes it possible to contemplate the expansion of infrastructure networks to reach previously unserved customers, and through the incentives provided by the competitive market to find innovative solutions to traditional infrastructure problems Affordability may be improved through significant cost reductions stemming from innovations and new managerial practices.

These benefits are likely to be particularly important in sectors where competition can be introduced, such as telecommunication services. In the other sectors, the effectiveness of reform in improving affordability will be driven largely by the effectiveness of the regulatory regime and its enforcement. In particular, a number of common features of infrastructure reform processes may adversely affect both access and affordability for the poor unless properly addressed by the regulatory environment. Access may be jeopardized by high initial costs of connection and by regulations that limit the availability of alternatives to conventional utility provision, and affordability may be affected by tariff reforms and the tightening of standards for quality of service.

Competition Rules and Regulatory Design

Competition rules and regulatory design are crucial in securing gains for the poor. Privatization is an important change, because it opens up access to private capital markets and introduces a profit motive in managing utilities. However, unless competition and regulation discipline the private sector operator, no guarantee exists that the profit motive will be harnessed to benefit customers, especially the poorest. Hence, the new model for infrastructure service provision that emerged during the 1990s is based on a clear institutional separation between the functions of policymaker, regulator, and service provider. In this model, the reform process itself consists of the following three main components:

- *Policies.* Policymakers typically decide on the restructuring of the service provider and the elimination of entry restrictions to open the way for competition wherever possible at the beginning of the reform process. This liberalization process requires some supervision from a competition agency responsible for ensuring that the potential efficiency gains are realized and that no abuses occur in the residual parts of the infrastructure services controlled by monopolies.
- *Regulation.* The function of regulatory agencies is to set tariffs and connection targets; monitor quality in the noncompetitive aspects of the service; and ensure that the efficiency gains achieved in the industry trickle down to all users, including the poor.
- *Provision.* The successful transfer of responsibility for service provision to private firms requires a fair distribution of risks between the firm, users, the government, and taxpayers. Recognizing these sources of risk is also important in the context of this study, as the poor, because of their limited ability to pay, are often regarded as a source of commercial risk, which can limit the attractiveness of deals to private operators. Managing this risk properly is therefore essential.

The distinction between these three components affects the choices of instruments a government can use to address the needs of the poor. Without a regulatory framework or without a government commitment to distinct rules of the game, few serious operators are likely to accept making significant investment commitments. The need to provide access and affordability to poor users must therefore be reconciled with the need to guarantee operators the expectation of a fair return on their investment. If this cannot be done, the government will generally be forced to rely on management contracts, limiting the risks to private operators, while itself financing the needed investment and consumption subsidies. With less access to private capital, the fiscal constraint becomes more binding and the choice of instruments is further restricted. Most of the suggestions made in this book are intended to minimize the risk of such a vicious circle.

2

Macroeconomic and Microeconomic Linkages between Infrastructure Reforms and Poverty

This chapter takes stock of the channels through which infrastructure reforms—especially private sector participation—influence poverty. We distinguish between macroeconomic and microeconomic linkages, because they reveal different types of policy issues and focus on different types of policy instruments. Both types of linkages have multiple facets that explain the diverse claims regarding the positive and negative effects of reform on poverty. The full picture is seldom exposed in debates, and analysts emphasize different linkages depending on whether reform, in particular private sector participation, is to be acclaimed or criticized. This overview of the literature tries to be as encompassing and as neutral as possible, yet remains incomplete because the evidence is still scarce. The experience with reform and private sector participation in most Latin American countries is also relatively recent and, with the exception of Chile and, to a lesser extent, Argentina, too recent to allow major conclusions. Preliminary findings in many countries, however, are substantive enough to provide relevant—albeit incomplete—insights.

Macroeconomic Linkages

Because infrastructure services account for a significant proportion of national income and consumption in many Latin American countries, any reform affecting the sector is likely to have wider repercussions for the economy as a whole. The infrastructure sectors typically account for 7.1 to

Table 2.1. *Macroeconomic Linkages between Infrastructure Reform and Poverty*

Category	Benefits	Risks
Economic growth	More private participation in infrastructure may help growth, and thereby poverty reduction, by increasing productivity and easing access to capital markets. In Latin America, a 1 percent growth in per capita GDP leads to a reduction of the share of the poor of close to half a percentage point.	If economic growth benefits mostly the nonpoor, poverty may not be reduced by much and inequality may increase, with a possible reduction in social welfare. Infrastructure reform can contribute to broadly based growth.
Employment	If infrastructure reform generates economic growth, there should ultimately be some employment creation, but it may take time.	Reforms may generate layoffs and reductions in wages, at least during the transition period. The negative impact of layoffs on poverty can be mitigated through severance packages and other policies.
Public expenditures	Revenues from reforms (for example, privatization) and the phasing out of subsidies generate fiscal space for other public programs that may be better targeted and more pro-poor.	The poor may be hurt by the reduction of public subsidies for infrastructure services (there may be cuts in the subsidies for both connections and consumption).

Source: Authors.

11 percent of GDP, including the transport sector, which accounts for 9 percent (World Bank 1994). From the perspective of the poor, three main macroeconomic issues are important, that is, the impact of privatization and infrastructure reform on economic growth, employment, and the composition of public expenditures (table 2.1).

Economic Growth

Because infrastructure services provide an important input into other commercial activities, the removal of infrastructure bottlenecks contributes to growth elsewhere in the economy. Table 2.2 summarizes studies relevant to Latin America. Two main channels contribute to the removal of bottle-necks. First, private sector participation, particularly when complemented by market liberalization and/or well-designed incentive regulation, can raise the size and the productivity of the infrastructure sector, and hence increase economic productivity. Second, access to private capital markets permits the financing of investments aimed at raising the quality of infra-structure services, as well as expanding overall capacity and increasing coverage levels.

The debate on the interactions between infrastructure and growth, in particular, the effects of infrastructure on productivity, has not been settled empirically. The evidence comes from two types of studies. The first fo-cuses on the absolute impact of infrastructure on macroeconomic produc-tion indicators. Aschauer (1989a,b) opened the debate by arguing that the elasticity of national GDP to infrastructure is high in the United States, roughly 0.4 for total public capital and 0.24 for core infrastructure. Munnell (1990a), Nadiri and Mamuneas (1994), and Wolff (1996) all confirm these results at the national level. However many researchers, including Garcia-Mila and McGuire (1992) and Morrison and Schwartz (1996), find this elas-ticity to be lower, and sometimes insignificant at the state or local level (Eberts 1990, Hulten and Schwab 1991). Munnell (1990b), for instance, finds it to be around 0.15 at the U.S. metropolitan level. The result has also been challenged on technical econometric grounds, but has not been settled (see de la Fuente 2000). Moreover, a flow of more rigorous studies now pro-vides evidence of the existence of a linkage between infrastructure and growth for other countries, including in Latin America. Baffes and Shah (1998) conclude that the elasticity of output to infrastructure is around 0.14 to 0.16 in Bolivia, Colombia, Mexico, and Venezuela. Ferreira (1996) finds an elasticity that varies between 0.34 and 1.122, depending on the discount rate used.

The second important way in which the influence of infrastructure on growth and poverty has been studied is through its effect on the conver-gence of regions. The literature has identified the key policy factors that can close the gap between regions within a country or across countries. In most studies, infrastructure is a key determinant of convergence and of reduction in disparity across regions. Detailed evidence exists for Argentina and Brazil, where improved access to sanitation and roads is a significant determinant of convergence for the poorest regions (Estache and Fay 1995).

One of the most painful lessons from the more technical literature is that unless governments take specific actions, the gains from reform take

Table 2.2. Macroeconomic Impact of Infrastructure Reforms and Government Failures

Source	Countries	Sectors	Reform	Method	Results
Galal and others (1994)	Chile, Malaysia, Mexico, United Kingdom	Electricity, tele- communiations, transport	Privatization	Construction of counterfactual based on pre-reform time series data. Projection of both actual and counterfactual scenarios into the future with the difference between the two providing the measure of welfare change. Impacts on owners, consumers, workers, and competitors explicitly modeled.	Substantial net welfare gains found in 11 of 12 case studies. Owners and workers generally gained from privatization. For consumers the results were more ambiguous, as consumers won in some cases and lost in others.
Estache and Fay (1995)	Argentina, Brazil	Electricity, roads, sanitation	Regional investment gaps	Regional relative and absolute convergence model ranking relative effect of various public investment programs on region- al growth.	Lack of infrastructure invest- ment revealed as main im- pediment to growth in several provinces in Argentina and states in Brazil.
Ferreira and Malliagros (1998)	Brazil	Infrastructure	Changes in public invest- ment programs and productivity	Econometric estimates of the linkages between infrastructure and GDP and total factor productivity.	Long-run output elasticity is 0.55–0.61, with the strongest effect coming from energy and transport; strong effect on total factor productivity as well.

Study	Country	Sector	Topic	Methodology	Findings
Baffes and Shah (1998)	Bolivia, Colombia, Mexico, Venezuela	Infrastructure	Public investment needs	Econometric analysis of elasticity of output to access to infrastructure.	Elasticity of output to infrastructure varies from 0.14 to 0.16.
Chisari, Estache, and Romero (1999) Navajas (2000)	Argentina	Electricity, gas, telecommunications, water	Privatization, regulation	General equilibrium model of the economy. Use of two alternative scenarios permits separate identification of the impact of privatization versus regulation.	Gains are equivalent to 2.25 percent of GDP, of which three-fourths are attributable to privatization and one-fourth to effective regulation. All income groups benefit, but the poor benefit more. The distribution of income improves. Macroeconomic indicators, including employment, also improve.
Alexander and Estache (2000)	Latin America	Electricity, gas, telecommunications, transport, water	Restructuring, privatization, regulation	Review of existing studies and compilation of case study material.	Evidence from a variety of sources indicates that reform of the infrastructure sector, when properly conducted, has a discernible impact on macroeconomic performance.
Benitez, Chisari, and Estache (2000)	Argentina	Electricity, gas, telecommunications, water	Privatization, fiscal reform, regulation	General equilibrium model of the economy to assess the fiscal consequences of utilities' privatization and regulation.	Shows that Argentina gains more from net present value of subsidy cuts and that largest share of increase in unemployment results from series of credit shocks rather than to utilities reform.

Source: Authors.

longer to reach the real poor than the richer segments of the population, and hence worsen income distribution. Recent evidence for Latin America indicates that the elasticity of the headcount index of poverty (the share of the population living in poverty) with respect to growth in per capita GDP is close to unity, even when the potential effects of growth on inequality are taken into account (Wodon 2001). With a headcount of poverty in Latin America of around 36 percent, a two percentage point increase in per capita GDP growth reduces the share of the population below the poverty line by about one percentage point.

Employment

Traditionally, public sector providers of infrastructure services have been characterized by substantial levels of overemployment. Indeed, state enterprises have often been consciously used as employment schemes, or even as informal social security systems. One of the most immediate consequences of private sector participation and reform is the shedding of labor with a view to raising the efficiency and profitability of infrastructure service providers. In Argentina the utilities' work force shrank from 300,000 in the 1980s to around 50,000 by 1993 (Alexander 2000). The extent to which the employment effects of private sector participation affect the poor depends on two factors. The first is the initial progressivity or regressivity in the distribution of employment in public enterprises, that is, whether the poor have access to public sector employment in infrastructure. The second critical issue is the compensation granted to workers laid off as a result of privatization. The size of "golden handshakes" and the generosity of retraining programs provided for those affected by privatization have varied considerably.

In the longer run, to the extent that sector reform contributes to economic growth, and thereby to new jobs, the initial layoffs in the public utilities may be compensated for by job creation in other sectors. This is one of the conclusions of simulations for Argentina by Benitez, Chisari, and Estache (2000); Chisari, Estache, and Romero (1999); and Navajas (2000). The studies use a general equilibrium model to calculate both sector-specific gains and the wider macroeconomic repercussions of private sector participation. They provide a breakdown of these gains across income quintiles and examine the effect of reform on the overall distribution of income in the economy. The Benitez, Chisari, and Estache (2000) study tests the relative impact of private sector participation and of credit market restrictions as alternative explanations for the increase in unemployment observed in Argentina. The test suggests that most of this increase can be attributed to credit rationing, refuting one of the standard myths associated with private sector participation.

Composition of Public Expenditures

Private sector participation and infrastructure reform can lead to a significant improvement in public finances. This reflects the elimination of subsidies, as well as the generation of privatization revenues. If these public funds are reallocated to programs whose incidence is more progressive than the original infrastructure connection investments and consumption subsidies, this change can benefit the poor. Vélez (1995) finds that in Colombia, subsidies for the consumption of utility services such as water, sewerage, electricity, and gas are substantially less progressive than public expenditures on health, education, and rural programs. Wodon, Ajwad, and Siaens (2000) obtain similar results for electricity subsidies in Honduras, with the nonpoor capturing most of the subsidies. Thus a shift in resources away from utility subsidies toward other programs may benefit lower-income groups. No guarantee exists, however, that public revenues will be reallocated in a pattern that is favorable to the poor.

While private sector participation tends to increase total welfare, the gains are not always shared with the poor. Galal and others (1994) estimate the welfare consequences of divestiture across a variety of sectors in Chile, Malaysia, Mexico, and the United Kingdom (see table 2.2). They focus on four stakeholder groups: the owners of the enterprises, the consumers, the workers, and the competitors. They construct a counterfactual "no divestiture" scenario based on projecting trends discernible in the five years before privatization. Welfare changes are then calculated relative to this benchmark. Both the actual and counterfactual scenarios are projected into the future to obtain the present value of the difference. This study retains a sectoral focus throughout without attempting to quantify the wider repercussions for economic growth and employment. For consumers, the welfare measure used is the change in consumer surplus. Although the study finds that the net welfare consequences of private sector participation are almost invariably positive overall, the picture for consumers is more ambiguous. In about half of the cases consumer welfare improves, and in the other half it deteriorates. The authors argue that the negative impacts are primarily attributable to prices being raised to efficient cost-recovery levels. However, the study does not distinguish between different types of consumers, such as the rich and the poor, nor is it clear how the authors handled the issue of estimating welfare for customers newly connected to the services or how they took changes in the quality of service into account.

Chisari, Estache, and Romero (1999) focus on private sector participation and regulation of the energy, telecommunications, and water sectors in Argentina. Their study also separates the benefits of private sector participation from those of effective regulation. According to the authors, private sector participation yielded operational gains in the infrastructure sectors equivalent to 0.90 percent of GDP, or 41 percent of average expenditure on utility services. Effective regulation added gains worth 0.35 percent of GDP (16 percent of the average expenditure on utility services). Higher-income households gained more in absolute terms than lower-income households, but the benefits of effective regulation as a proportion of existing expenditures on utility services were highest for the lowest income quintiles. This is because regulation acts as a mechanism for transferring rents from the owners of capital to the consumers of the service. Overall, according to the simulations, the Gini coefficient of income inequality fell by –0.24 points as a result of private sector participation when regulation is effective.

Ultimately, the growth-infrastructure access interaction is a two-way affair. While infrastructure reform may help to boost growth, growth itself is a key determinant of access to services. However, it is not the only determinant, and may not be the most important one. Ryan and Wodon (2001) find that urbanization affects access to infrastructure services and other social indicators more than it affects growth. For extremely poor countries, one percentage point of growth results in a 0.338 percent (not percentage point) increase in access to safe water and a 0.668 percent increase in telephone main lines per 100 inhabitants. As GDP improves, the impact of growth vanishes, but the impact of urbanization remains strong as urbanization increases. Overall, urbanization has a large effect on access to basic infrastructure services, and in some cases more than economic growth.

Microeconomic Linkages

Just as in the case of macroeconomic linkages, the microeconomic linkages can be organized into two groups: linkages that affect access to infrastructure services, such as rising connection costs and dwindling availability of alternative sources of supply, and those that affect the affordability of the service for those who have access, such as increasing formalization, rising prices, changing tariff structures, and rising quality standards (table 2.3). In some cases, linkages can affect both access and affordability, but the conceptual distinction is still useful, because the policy instruments tend to be tailored to address them separately.

Table 2.3. *Microeconomic Linkages between Infrastructure Reform and the Poor*

Category	Risks	Benefits and mitigating factors
Access issues		
Increase in connection fees	The fee for obtaining a connection to the infrastructure service is likely to increase substantially when privatized firms reflect actual costs of connections.	Countries can adopt rules to ensure that connection costs are uniform across geographic areas.
Risk of "cream-skimming" or "red-lining"	Firms may have incentives not to serve the poor on an individual (cream-skimming) or neighborhood (red-lining) basis.	Rules against cream-skimming or red-lining can be imposed.
Reduction in the availability of alternative services	The fee for obtaining a connection to the infrastructure service is likely to increase substantially when privatized firms reflect actual costs of connections.	Access to alternative services will not be affected if foreseen in contracts. Availability of communal services may increase as a result of privatization.
Increase in network cost caused by service quality upgrades	The quality of service is likely to improve, but this may make network services unaffordable for the poor.	Evidence shows that poor households are willing to pay reasonable amounts to improve the quality of service.
Consumption affordability issues		
Increase in pricing	Average tariff levels can increase because of cost-recovery requirements and the need to finance quality-related investments.	Increases in average tariffs depend on pre-reform price levels and the distribution of the benefits of private participation between stakeholders. Reform can cut costs significantly through improvements in efficiency or new technologies.
Tariff rebalancing	Tariff structure is likely to be reformed in ways that could increase the marginal tariff faced by the poor.	Competition is likely to decrease average tariffs, thereby possibly compensating for the impact of tariff rebalancing.
Formalization and revenue collection	Revenue collection and discouragement of informal connections are likely to be more effective and result in an increase in the effective price paid.	A formal connection, even at a cost, may be desired by vulnerable households. Safety is likely to increase with the formalization of connections. Informal connection may have been more expensive. Reform can bring technology choices that lower costs.

Source: Authors.

Access Issues

Three main types of access issues can result from infrastructure reform and private sector participation:

- Potential increases in initial connection fees
- Reluctance of operators to serve the poor
- Reduction in the availability of alternative sources of supply.

Whereas the investment costs of state-owned enterprises were typically subsidized, privately-operated utilities often charge substantial one-time connection (or infrastructure) charges to cover the costs of network expansion. High connection charges for water and sewerage proved an obstacle to service expansion in Buenos Aires. The concession contract enabled firms to charge new customers the cost of the connection plus part of the costs of expanding the secondary network, a total of $1,100 to $1,500 per connection spread over 24 monthly installments. Many unconnected customers lived in areas with an average household income of about $245 a month, and thus were asked to contribute a monthly installment of around 20 percent of their annual income to get a connection.

More generally, households may have to make significant investments in wiring or plumbing their homes over and above connection charges to reap the full benefits of an infrastructure connection. These costs can be prohibitively high for low-income customers, preventing them from connecting to a network once it has been built. Reform processes must take into account the potential obstacles access costs pose and find ways to reduce them.

Private operators have no incentives to serve customers whose cost of provision exceeds the tariff that they pay. Poor customers are relatively costly to serve for several reasons. First, higher commercial risk and billing costs may be associated with recovering revenues from customers with limited ability to pay. Second, as poor neighborhoods are often located in topographically difficult sites, this can increase the technical complexity of providing infrastructure services. Finally, poor households often consume relatively small quantities of the service, meaning that the fixed costs of service provision are spread over a relatively small number of units of demand. Cross-subsidies may exacerbate this problem by reducing the amount of revenue that can be collected, thereby making poor households even more commercially unattractive to serve. Thus once competition is introduced, new entrants may be tempted to "'cream-skim," or acquire only customers whose tariffs exceed their true cost of provision, leaving the incumbent with customers who are uneconomic to serve. One form of this is "red-lining," where whole neighborhoods or geographic areas enjoy service while other areas, typically less profitable, are essentially ignored unless governments are willing to subsidize the operators.

A substantial proportion of the poorest households lack access to conventional utility connections and consequently must find substitutes to meet their needs for water, sanitation, energy, and communication. These include self-supply, communal supply, non-network alternatives, and alternative networks (see table 2.4). Ironically, the private sector provides many of these substitute services, so that privatization is already a reality for the poorest households. For these customers, sector reform represents less a transition from public to private sector provision than from informal to formal private sector provision. Because the poor often rely on substitutes to conventional utility services, defining the role of alternative suppliers is an integral

Table 2.4. *Examples of Substitutes to Conventional Utilities for Infrastructure Services*

Substitute	Energy	Telecommunications	Water and sanitation
Self-supply	Collection of firewood	n.a.	Collection of surface water, construction of wells, "natural" disposal of excreta
Communal supply	Street lighting	Fixed public telephones, mobile public telephones	Public standpipes, public toilets
Alternative non-network suppliers	Photovoltaic cells, candles, kerosene, batteries	Resale of telephony, pagers, mobile telephones, voice mail services	Tanker supplies, bottled water, resale of piped water, septic tanks and latrines
Alternative network suppliers	Informal networks	n.a.	Informal networks

n.a. Not applicable.
Source: Authors.

part of any sector reform strategy (Erhardt 2000), if only because universal access to conventional network utilities cannot be achieved overnight. The transition period toward full conventional coverage may last for many years, and during this period ensuring that the substitute services function as adequately as possible is important. Yet in some cases alternative forms of provision may actually be or become illegal after the reforms (Kariuki and Acolor 2000, Kariuki and Wandera 2000). In other cases alternative suppliers, though legal, may face unfair competition from the conventional utility. This is even more damaging when substitute services provide a cost-quality balance more closely suited to the needs of the poor than conventional utilities or when they provide competitive pressure for the conventional utility to reduce its charges.

In the water sector, regulatory frameworks typically outlaw self-supply, resale of piped water, and alternative distribution networks, for several reasons. First, for private operators to finance substantial investments in network expansion, some guarantee of demand is typically provided via exclusivity clauses that require all customers with access to the network to make a household connection. Second, alternative suppliers may give rise to undesirable health or environmental consequences (such as the supply of nonpotable water or exploitation of an aquifer by numerous unregulated wells). Third, households that lack a household connection pay substantially higher rates to purchase water from alternative sources. Still, as mentioned earlier, preventing alternative suppliers from operating may not be the best option for the poor.

The situation is different in the telecommunications sector, because market liberalization and the growth of mobile telephony services almost automatically increase the range of alternative suppliers providing services.

In general, electricity sector reforms do not greatly affect the availability of alternative providers, either in the positive sense of encouraging entry or in the negative sense of granting exclusivity to electricity distributors. Non-network alternatives to electricity represent a relatively high-cost solution, so customers may have a strong incentive to connect to the grid. A study in Guatemala (Foster, Tre, and Wodon, 2000a,b) found that, considering the differential luminous efficacy of kerosene and electricity, the cost of illuminating a household in 1998 with simple wick-based kerosene lamps was $5.87 per kilowatt hour of effective energy output, versus $0.08 per kilowatt hour for electricity. In practice, providing electricity to remote households in rural areas may be too expensive, and promoting cheaper alternative suppliers may be an important component of reform.

Affordability Issues

Reform and private sector participation can give rise to the following four broad sources of affordability restrictions:

- Tariff increases needed to cover costs
- Increase in costs caused by required increases in service quality standards
- Tariff rebalancing needed to reduce cross-subsidies
- Formalization of payment for usage.

Although reform has the potential to reduce the costs of service provision, the price to the customer may increase, at least in the short term. Because of political considerations, many publicly-owned utilities have charged tariffs that fall well short of the true economic costs of provision. A key objective of reform is to make infrastructure services financially self-sustaining, and therefore tariff increases may be required. The extent to which prices rise or fall because of private sector participation, however, is to some extent a political choice. The impact of a reform process on prices depends partly on pre-reform cost and tariff levels, but also on how the benefits of privatization are distributed among stakeholders.

Governments have a choice between fixing a relatively high tariff and then auctioning off the operator on the basis of the highest royalty payment, or waiving the royalty payment altogether and auctioning off the service to the party who bids the lowest service tariff. In one case, the government directly appropriates efficiency gains made by the private operator, whereas in the other they go directly to consumers. In the first case, high tariffs can be viewed as a tax on consumers to fund the fiscal deficit through a high sale value of the company rather than because of privatization. A recent survey of 600 concession contracts from around the world found that in most cases contracts are tendered for the highest transfer or annual fee, suggesting that governments are more concerned with relieving fiscal constraints than securing tariff reductions (Guasch 2000).

In the constrained fiscal environment of the 1990s, many governments in Latin America saw utility reform as a golden opportunity to stop the growing drain of state subsidies to the utility services and to replenish the public coffers with the revenue generated by the sale of state-owned enterprises. Thus, as shown in figure 2.1, of the $290 billion of private sector investment flowing to infrastructure projects in Latin America during 1990–99, $170 billion (about 58 percent) went to governments as divestiture revenues rather than being invested directly into the sector (Izaguirre and Rao 2000).

Figure 2.1. *Breakdown of Private Capital Flows to Developing Countries, by Region, 1990–99*

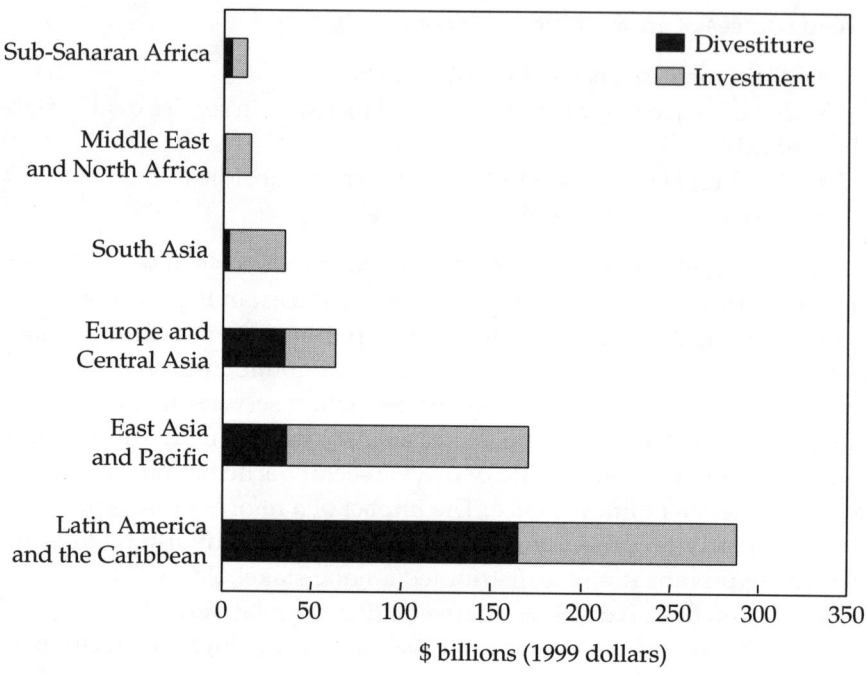

Source: Izaguirre and Rao (2000).

The equivalent proportion for the rest of the developing world is much lower, around 27 percent. The East Asia and Pacific region attracted a much smaller overall volume of private investment than Latin America ($170 billion versus $290 billion), but achieved a higher level of direct investment in the infrastructure sectors ($134 billion versus $122 billion).

A major source of dissatisfaction with state-owned utilities has been the low quality of service provided, particularly in terms of supply interruptions and service rationing. Improving the quality of service often requires significant investments to upgrade and expand the capacity of the network. This will be reflected in higher tariffs, which may be detrimental to the poor. The balance between quality and tariffs imposed by the regulator on a private provider may be based on standards valid for the average customer but not for the poor. Differentiating quality standards between classes of customers may be necessary to provide better value to the poor.

Tariff structures operated by state-owned utilities typically embody a complex array of cross-subsidies between different customer groups. These may include cross-subsidies between different services (such as water and sewerage), different sectors (such as domestic and commercial), different geographical areas (such as urban and rural), and different levels of consumption. Because existing cross-subsidies are often socially motivated, their removal may be detrimental to the poor. Perhaps the clearest example comes from the telecommunications sector, where historically long-distance charges have been artificially inflated to reduce the cost of local telephone calls for social reasons. Such cross-subsidies are unsustainable once competition is introduced in long-distance telephony, so that rebalancing local and long-distance charges is often an integral component of telecommunications sector reform. To the extent that the poor tend to make more local calls than long-distance calls, they may be adversely affected. Nonetheless, this concern is premised on the assumption that existing cross-subsidies are effective in reaching the poor. As shown later, this is not always the case. Where cross-subsidies fail to reach the poor, dismantling them should not pose any serious concern.

Because of weak commercial incentives and the unwillingness to disconnect service, state-owned enterprises often failed to collect the tariff revenue owed them. Thus many customers effectively received the service free. Private operators, however, usually crack down on network theft in the form of illegal connections or fraudulent meters, another means of receiving the service free.

Vélez (1995) estimates that the implicit subsidy from nonpayment by informal or illegal connections in Colombia's urban centers in 1992 accounted for 6 percent of all subsidies in the electricity sector and 24 percent of all subsidies in water and sanitation. In the gas sector, formally connected households paid a surcharge over costs, and nonpaying households received an implicit subsidy. Overall, illegal connections or nonpayment accounted for close to 9 percent of all subsidies in the gas, electricity, and water sector in Colombia in 1992. Illegal or informal connections were more common among poor households, with most of the implicit subsidies benefiting the poorer half of the population. The elimination of such implicit subsidies will have a negative effect on the poor if not compensated for by other measures. That is, with better revenue collection after privatization, many poor customers find themselves forced to pay for the service for the first time.

However, in some countries the poorest formally unconnected users have illegal connections from illegal providers, but pay these illegal providers rates equivalent to formal operator charges. In the Dominican Republic, the poor commonly pay flat fees for illegal connections. The recent privatization of electricity distribution does not affect costs to the poor, because the poor were previously paying informal operators an amount equivalent to their current bills. In such cases, the introduction of a formal operator concerned with cost recovery may provide the poor with an additional option, and competition between the private utility and the informal suppliers may end up lowering tariffs for the poorest.

Policy Implications

The macroeconomic and microeconomic linkages between infrastructure reform and the poor are far from straightforward. Policy failures can hurt the poor in multiple ways. Policy coordination that considers the needs of the poor is critical during infrastructure reform, especially in relation to reform that includes private sector participation in services in which prices are expected to reflect both operating and capital costs.

Two sources of difficulty exist for infrastructure reformers. The first and probably more important is that many of the mitigating policy actions that policymakers could consider to improve access and affordability are not directly under their control. Credit rationing, for instance, is likely to hurt a sector with large, long-lived investment requirements, but infrastructure ministers cannot do much without the support of the finance minister. Support is needed to substitute for the market when the private cost of capital imposed by the market is overwhelmingly higher than the cost of public capital. More generally, mitigating solutions will often require some type of subsidy, which requires a fiscal commitment that many governments prefer to avoid, even when it is the only way to help the poor. Reform requires the commitment of the whole government, not just the infrastructure minister.

A second challenge for policy reformers is publicizing that positive effects often compensate for possible negative effects of reform on affordability. The reform often results in a different service bundle that includes better quality and, in particular, safer service. Deaths related to improper handling of illegally connected wires, for instance, demonstrate the dangers of informal electric connections. Illegal connections for water may reduce water quality. In such cases, if the household is aware of and values the extra health and safety benefits of a formal connection, this household may perceive that these additional benefits compensate for the increase in tariffs.

This is confirmed by willingness to pay surveys in Central and South America (Walker and others 2000). These surveys indicate that even very poor households would prefer to pay a reasonable bill to have a formal connection to piped water services instead of maintaining an informal connection. Apart from health concerns, this may be partly because of the uncertainty regarding continued access to the service with an informal or illegal connection. In some cases, being a formal customer of a utility and being able to present a water or electricity bill may be necessary to obtain other state benefits or to deal with the state bureaucracy. For urban households who live in recently created shanty towns without proper land titles, a formal connection to a utility, even at a cost, may be a first step toward formal ownership of the property.

3

Promoting Access

When designing infrastructure reforms aimed at the needs of the poor, a government must first assess their degree of access to infrastructure services. This can sometimes be a challenge, because the necessary data sets are not always available. This chapter reviews the information available, proposes new indicators of access, and discusses the policy instruments that reformers could consider to improve access where and when needed in the context of increased private sector participation.

Trends in Access Rates

Total access rates in Latin America are growing, but slowly. Table 3.1 provides estimates of access rates for 22 Latin American countries for 1986–96 based on international datasets. The nonweighted trend represents population-based access rates and may be distorted by a few populous countries. The trend assigning equal weight to all countries can be used to assess the performance of governments and private providers in providing access. Both trends yield similar results and show some improvement in access rates in Latin America during the period. By far the most dramatic increase has been in teledensity, which virtually doubled during the decade.

International data sets may overstate access, however. Global databases include information on access to safe water and sanitation, as well as telephone main lines per 100 inhabitants, but because the measures in these databases do not exactly correspond to the concept of a household connection, they may overstate the level of coverage as explained below.

- *Water.* Coverage is defined as the share of the population with reasonable access to an adequate amount of safe water, including treated

Table 3.1. *Access to Electricity, Water, and Telephone in 22 Latin American Countries Based on International Datasets, Selected Years, 1986–96*

	Weighted				Nonweighted			
Year	Water	Sanitation	Telephone	Electricity	Water	Sanitation	Telephone	Electricity
1986	75.99	66.99	5.46	82.19	68.34	73.63	4.58	72.16
1989	80.85	79.85	6.13	85.37	69.88	77.21	5.23	76.25
1992	81.33	79.84	7.44	87.72	70.16	77.50	6.54	80.19
1995	—	79.65	9.41	89.37	73.19	79.67	8.54	81.76
1996	—	—	10.30	90.10	—	—	9.42	80.91

— Not available.

Note: The water estimate with weights drops in 1995 because of data for Brazil, which may not be reliable.

Source: Authors.

    surface water and untreated but uncontaminated water, such as from springs, sanitary wells, and protected boreholes. In urban areas, the source may be a public fountain or standpost located not more than 200 meters away from the dwelling. This definition means that members of the household do not have to spend a disproportionate part of the day fetching water. An adequate amount of water needed to satisfy metabolic, hygienic, and domestic requirements is usually about 20 liters of safe water per person per day. The definition of safe water has changed over time, however.

- *Sanitation.* Coverage refers to the share of the population with excreta disposal facilities that can effectively prevent human, animal, and insect contact with excreta. Suitable facilities range from simple but protected pit latrines to flush toilets with sewerage. To be regarded as effective, all facilities must be correctly constructed and properly maintained.

- *Telephone.* Coverage is defined in terms of the number of telephone main lines per 100 inhabitants. Because many of these lines are used for commercial purposes, this indicator overstates the household connection rate.

    The Latin American trends presented in appendix 3.1 at the end of this chapter reflect the results of household surveys from 12 countries, which are summarized in table 3.2. National data are available for some countries, including Brazil and Mexico, but only urban data are available for others.

The surveys cover three-fourths of the Latin American population. The data on electricity and water are reliable in most surveys, but only a few surveys have information on telephone access and sewerage. The Latin American average is computed both with and without country weights, with the country weights based on the population represented in the surveys. As in table 3.1, the two trends are similar, and discussion focuses on the trends with weights.

One benefit of the household surveys is that they allow us to distinguish between urban and rural families. A number of lessons emerge from an analysis of the household surveys. First, access to electricity is nearly universal in urban areas, although some urban populations living in slums may not be well represented in the household surveys. In rural areas, the coverage rate increased from 60 to 70 percent between 1986 and 1996, still far from universal. With Latin America's population of 486 million people in 1996, an overall connection rate of 90.1 percent and an average household size of five people among the poor, the access deficit is about 10 million connections, mostly in rural areas.

Second, 9 out of 10 people in urban areas have a connection to water, versus only half of the population in rural areas. In both urban and rural areas access rates increased by five percentage points between 1986 and 1996. With an overall Latin American access rate of 81.1 percent, the deficit in the number of connections is estimated at 18 million.

Third, because the data in the surveys are weaker for telephone access, we do not provide a Latin American trend. Appendix 3.1 shows, however, that coverage is increasing. In Mexico, for example, national coverage increased from 15.8 to 26.5 percent in 1996.

While aggregate access rates may seem reasonable by developing country standards, the household-level data reveal that significant inequalities in access exist among services across urban and rural areas and between rich and poor, although there is evidence that inequality has been decreasing over time (see appendix 3.2). Electricity is the infrastructure service with the highest access rate, and therefore the most egalitarian pattern of access, followed by water. Telephone and sewerage connections are distributed much more inequitably. The countries with the highest level of access have the lowest inequality in access. In other words, both coverage and equality in access in the low-income countries (for example, Bolivia, Guatemala, and Honduras) lag substantially behind those observed in the middle-income countries (for instance, Brazil, Chile, Colombia, and Mexico). For all services, inequality of access is substantially greater in rural than in urban areas, again because access levels are higher in urban areas.

Table 3.2. Access to Electricity and Water in 12 Latin American Countries Based on National Household Surveys, Selected Years, 1986–96

Year	Electricity						Water					
	National		Urban		Rural		National		Urban		Rural	
	With weight	Without weight	With weight	Without weight	With weight	Without weight	With weight	Without weight	With weight	Without weight	With weight	Without weight
1986	82.19	72.16	95.51	92.43	59.26	54.21	72.05	66.24	86.87	84.57	46.76	51.72
1989	85.37	76.25	96.77	94.68	65.20	58.39	74.54	71.01	87.82	85.42	49.82	52.11
1992	87.72	80.19	97.23	95.45	66.13	61.53	76.74	75.02	88.58	87.03	48.58	50.81
1995	89.37	81.76	97.96	95.66	68.24	63.75	78.81	75.41	90.76	88.17	49.08	50.92
1996	90.10	80.91	98.21	96.81	69.89	60.77	81.14	75.74	92.36	88.85	51.80	48.95

Source: Authors; Wodon and Ajwad (2000a).

Time Frame of Benefits

Despite the data quality problems, the available data can be used to esti-mate how the access rate would improve over the next 20 years without any major change in policy. A rough forecast can be made that reflects the likely effect of growth and continued urbanization. Figure 3.1 provides pro-jections for future levels of access to safe water and telephones in Latin America. Using a growth rate of per capita GDP of 2 percent per year and an extrapolation of the historical trend for urbanization (the two factors identified as being key determinants of access rates), telephone density can be expected to quadruple by 2020. Access to safe water, however, will im-prove more slowly (albeit from a higher initial level). If these assumptions are reasonable, raising access to safe water in Latin America from its cur-rent 75 percent to beyond the 90 percent level may take an additional 20 years. In the same time span, telephone penetration could reach 40 main lines per 100 inhabitants, although technological progress may further the process for this sector.

Given that 20 years from now, coverage is still unlikely to be universal, focusing only on the trend may be insufficient to predict if the poor will

Figure 3.1. *Projection of Water and Telephone Access for the Latin American Region, 1995–2019*

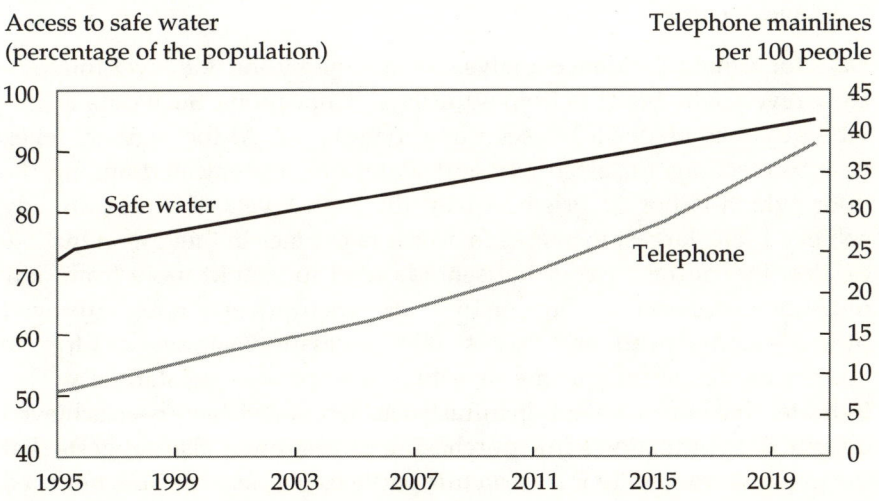

Source: Based on Ryan and Wodon (2001).

gain from the coverage increases anticipated in the medium run. Conceptually, policymakers should be concerned mainly with identifying who will benefit from further increases to access that result from a policy change. One quick way to determine the incidence of the expected increase is to perform a combined analysis of the data on access levels provided earlier and the concentration coefficients. This suggests that the higher the overall level of access, the lower the inequality in access, meaning that, on average, the poor do indeed benefit from any improvement. This is simply because once the rich have gained access, which they do first by virtue of their location and wealth, increases in access rates automatically benefit the poor.

To obtain a more reliable assessment requires a more analytical approach. In this context, marginal incidence analysis (who benefits from increases in connections) is more important than standard incidence analysis (how current connections are distributed), because public policies tend to have an impact at the margin. Hence, marginal incidence is the appropriate approach for evaluating alternative policies.

Two approaches are available to determine who benefits from additional connections. The first is to look at the distributional incidence of new connections made over time using time series data. The alternative, when only a single cross-section of data is available, is to study patterns of access across geographical areas at a specific point in time.

Time Series Data

Data for benefit incidence analysis over time by income level immediately reveal who benefits from additional connections. Such data is provided by income decile, as seen in appendix 3.2. At the regional level, new connections for electricity and water are concentrated among the poor, which is not surprising given the high levels of access already achieved. The largest increases in access take place in the lowest income deciles. By contrast, richer households tend to benefit more from new telephone connections. During 1986–96, when poverty rates improved little (Wodon, Ajwad, and Siaens 2000), access to basic services for the bottom deciles of the income distribution improved substantially. This indicates that improvements in infrastructure coverage have been achieved despite the population's low purchasing power, but it also suggests that the improved access to infrastructure services has, as expected, not been enough to lift people out of poverty.

Single Cross-Section

With only a single cross-section of data, looking at marginal benefit incidence analysis with special methods is still feasible (see box 3.1). Table 3.3 presents results for Bolivia. An estimate of marginal benefit incidence larger (smaller) than one indicates that the corresponding group benefits more (less) than other groups from a national expansion of the service. In Bolivia, new connections remain skewed toward richer municipalities, except for water. Nevertheless, the differences in marginal incidence are smaller than the differences in incidence, confirming that when coverage improves, the poor benefit more than before from new connections.

Who Has Gained Access?

While marginal benefit incidence is useful to compare the distribution of new connections across income classes, improved access seldom takes place in a policy vacuum. This is particularly relevant when considering the effects of infrastructure strategies in Latin America. Although frequently used, raw data on connections before and after reform are not a good basis on which to assess the impact of reform on access rates, because they result from multiple policy decisions or environmental variables. In Argentina and Chile connection rates in electricity and telecommunications services improved significantly after private sector participation, yet determining how much of this expansion was due to private sector participation is difficult, because other important economic changes took place during this period (such as the growth in disposable income and changes in the pricing and regulation of these services). Evaluating the impact of reform on access rates is even more difficult in other countries where reform took place more recently, because of the scarcity of postreform data.

From a policy viewpoint, the main purpose of finding out who benefits from reform is to help policymakers fine-tune policies and address areas of concern. For renegotiations or arbitration, for instance, being aware how much some categories of users have been hurt may be useful. The redesign of the water concession contract in Buenos Aires, Argentina, illustrates the type of adjustment that may be suggested once the private operator comes to know its customer base after a few months of operation. In that case, the poorest consumers were the main victims of the new tariff design for the connection, because with the new tariff structure, connections were

---

Box 3.1. *Marginal Benefit Incidence Analysis with a Single Cross-Section*

Consider a country with $i = 1, \ldots$, with N departments. Within each department, the municipalities are ranked by a measure of per capita income. That is, the municipalities are assigned to one of $q = 1, \ldots, Q$ intervals in their department, and the same number of intervals Q is used in each department. Denote by x^q_{ij} the value of social indicator x in municipality j belonging to interval q of department i. The mean benefit incidence in interval q for department i is denoted by X^q_i and J^q_i is the number of municipalities in interval q of department i. To assess how various groups (that is, intervals) of municipalities benefit from an improvement in the social indicator, we run Q regressions:

$$X^q_i = \alpha^q + \beta^q \left(\frac{\sum_{q=1, j=1}^{Q, J^q_i} x^q_{ij} - \sum_{j=1}^{J^q_i} x^q_{ij}}{\sum_{q=1}^{Q} J^q_i - J^q_i} \right) + \varepsilon^q_i \qquad \text{for } q = 1, \ldots, Q.$$

For the poorest interval ($q = 1$), this yields a regression of the level X^1_i of the indicator in the poorest municipalities in the various departments on the mean level of the indicator in the departments as a whole. One caveat exists: to avoid the problem of endogeneity (standard department means are obtained over all the municipalities in the department, including those in the first interval), the right-hand variable is computed at the departmental level as the mean on all municipalities except those belonging to interval q. With this setting, the marginal increase for the indicator in interval q is $Q\beta^q/(Q-1 + \beta^q)$, where Q is the total number of intervals. The sum of these marginal impacts must be equal to Q. To estimate the parameters β^q immediately, one could pool the data and run a single regression where the intercepts and slopes are allowed to differ between intervals:

$$X^q_i = \sum_{q=1}^{Q} \alpha^q + \sum_{q=1}^{Q} \beta^q \left(\frac{\sum_{q=1}^{Q} X^q_i - X^q_i}{Q - 1} \right) + \varepsilon^q_i.$$

However, there is a restriction in the estimation of this regression, in that the sum of all marginal effects $\sum_{q=1}^{Q} \dfrac{\beta^q}{Q - 1 + \beta^q} = 1$ must be Q. Writing β^Q in terms of the other parameters yields

(box continues on following page)

Box 3.1. *(continued)*

$$\beta^Q = \frac{(Q-1)\left(1 - \sum_{q=1}^{Q-1} \dfrac{\beta^q}{Q-1+\beta^q}\right)}{\sum_{q=1}^{Q-1} \dfrac{\beta^q}{Q-1+\beta^q}}.$$

This restriction can be taken into account through nonlinear least squares estimation.

Source: Ajwad and Wodon (2000); Wodon and Ajwad (2000a). See also Lanjouw and Ravallion (1999).

unaffordable. Everyone recognized that some adjustment to the formula was needed, and the focus of the discussion between regulators, operators, and users was clear.

Not all adjustment needs are as easy to identify. Users have a strong incentive to complain that they are worse off to try to minimize their utility bills. Any regulator or policymakers trying to be fair will need analytical support to guide decisions where opportunities arise to change the rules of the game to allow increased connections among the poor. Because regulatory accounting controls continue to be weak throughout most of Latin America and tariff changes are often one of many changes reform brings, policymakers must rely on "back of the envelope" approaches that can shed some light and help them make fair decisions.

One approach that can be used to assess the impact of reform on access rates is building a counterfactual. Most policymakers have enough information to compare residential and industrial users. This analytical approach—described in detail in box 3.2—can be used to assess the effects of the 1995 electricity reform in Bolivia. The idea is to test whether differences exist in the treatment of residential and industrial customers after the reform, and whether these differences show if the operators are giving priority to industrial customers, possibly at a cost to residential customers (due to tariff rebalancing, for example). By comparing how residential and

Table 3.3. *Who Benefits from Service Expansion, Bolivia*

Service	Estimates of the marginal benefit incidence by municipal income group			Tests of differences in the marginal benefit incidence estimates (p-values, 5% level)		
	Poor	*Middle*	*Rich*	*Poor versus middle*	*Middle versus rich*	*Poor versus rich*
Water	0.937	1.124	0.940	No	No	No
Sewage	0.219	0.881	1.900	Yes	Yes	Yes
Electricity	0.504	1.355	1.141	Yes	No	Yes
Garbage collection	0.534	0.687	1.779	No	Yes	Yes
Telephone	0.305	0.654	2.041	No	Yes	Yes

Source: Ajwad and Wodon (2000).

industrial consumers have fared before and after the privatization, one can hope to control for influences that affect both groups of customers, such as a reduction in the cost of producing energy.

The results are reported in table 3.4. The first part of the table shows the effects of changes in prices and connection on consumer surplus (that is, an improvement in welfare) for every period. The bottom part of the table provides the tests as to whether there is a difference before and after 1995 in the welfare gains. For residential customers, a minor difference exists, while there is no difference for industrial customers. This suggests that industrial customers were better protected, but the loss to residential customers was small.

Overall, this calculation shows that making blanket statements about the incidence of infrastructure reform is difficult. The context and scope of reform leading to changes in access rates are different in every country, and often in every sector. Methods that explicitly model reforms (such as general equilibrium methods in Benitez, Chisari, and Estache 2000; Chisari, Estache, and Romero 1999; Navajas 2000) are probably the most complete, but are generally too demanding in terms of data. The methodology proposed here is far from perfect, but it can generate useful insights that may guide a decision for a regulator with a mandate to assess the distributional effects of increased rates of connection achieved through reform.

Box 3.2. *Impact of Privatization on Access Rates and Prices in Bolivia*

To quantify the welfare impacts of privatization on electricity consumers in Bolivia, Ajwad, Anguizola, and Wodon (2000) use data on electricity prices and new connections for residential and industrial customers by electric utility for 1992–98. This time frame permits a comparison of price and connection tendencies for both residential and industrial customers immediately before (1992–95) and after privatization (1995–98). The welfare impact of changes in prices and connection rates are quantified by calculating the change in consumer surplus as a percentage of total expenditure on electricity for the average consumer. Denote the change in consumer surplus by ΔCS; total per capita consumption by C; the share of expenditures allocated to electricity in period one by S_1; the electricity prices in real terms in period one and two by p_1 and p_2, respectively; and the price elasticity of demand for electricity by e. To assess impacts on welfare, we compute the change in consumer surplus as a percentage of total expenditures before and after privatization. Assuming that demand for electricity is linear in price, we have

$$ Y = \frac{\Delta CS}{C} = S_1 \left[\frac{(p_1 - p_2)}{p_1} \right] \left[1 + \frac{e(p_1 - p_2)}{2p_1} \right]. $$

Using a regional data set for 1992–98, Y is computed for each of Bolivia's regions and each year for changes in prices and connections. For the households that are connected, all the variables above are observed except elasticity e. To test for robustness, we compute the changes in welfare with elasticities equal to zero and one. To estimate the gains in welfare associated with a new connection to the electricity grid for the households not connected, we assume that the connection results in a 25 percent decrease in the cost of energy for newly connected households (Foster, Tre, and Wodon 2000a; Wodon, Ajwad, and Siaens 2000). Panel fixed effects regressions are then estimated as follows:

$$ Y_{it} = \alpha_i + \gamma_t + \varepsilon_{it}. $$

In these regressions, each of Bolivia's departments has a different intercept α_i, but we are more interested in the time effects γ_t. The parameter estimates can be interpreted as changes in consumer surplus associated with different years. If the estimates for the time effects decrease after the privatization, we interpret the results as an indication that privatization has been associated with welfare gains; if the estimates increase, losses are indicated. That is, if T is the total number of years for which we have observations, and if P denotes the year of the privatization, we test whether

(box continues on following page)

Box 3.2. *(continued)*

$$\sum_{t=1}^{P} \frac{\gamma_t}{P} \neq \sum_{t=P+1}^{T} \frac{\gamma_t}{T-P}.$$

The evidence suggests that for residential customers, the increases in consumer surplus generated by both the decrease in real prices and by new connections were larger in the beginning of the sample period than in the end. This is not observed for industrial customers. After the privatization, industrial customers were better protected than residential customers. Still, there was no drastic drop in consumer surplus for residential customers after the privatization. Given that the government increased social spending using in part the savings from the privatization process, overall privatization seems not to have had a negative welfare impact.

Source: Ajwad, Anguizola, and Wodon (2000).

Table 3.4. *Percentage Increase in Welfare for Changes in Electricity Prices and Connections, Bolivia, 1992–98*

	Residential (%)				Industrial (%)			
	Elasticity = 0		Elasticity = –1		Elasticity = 0		Elasticity = –1	
Year	Price	Connec-tion	Price	Connec-tion	Price	Connec-tion	Price	Connec-tion
1992–93	0.452	1.693	0.480	1.917	NS	1.452	NS	1.632
1993–94	0.413	1.626	0.452	1.846	NS	1.297	NS	1.475
1994–95	NS	1.399	NS	1.565	NS	1.585	0.521[a]	1.874
1995–96	0.326	1.556	0.341	1.748	0.511	1.704	0.563[a]	1.949
1996–97	NS	1.281	NS	1.415	NS	1.334	NS	1.488
1997–98	NS	1.386	NS	1.543	NS	1.496	NS	1.680
Test for change	0.06	0.10	0.07	0.06	NS	NS	NS	NS
after privatiza-		0.02		0.01		NS		NS
tion (p value)								

NS Not statistically different from zero at the 10 percent level.
Note: Coefficients are significant at 5 percent level. For the test, when significant, the level of significance is directly indicated.
[a] Significant at 10 percent.
Source: Ajwad, Anguizola, and Wodon (2000).

Instruments to Improve or Facilitate Access

Whether policymakers are preparing a new reform or trying to fine-tune an existing reform to improve access for the poorest, they may use various types of instruments. Table 3.5 provides a detailed list of instruments with their advantages and disadvantages. None of these alternatives should be regarded as mutually exclusive, and successful examples from Latin America discussed in the following sections combine several of these instruments. These instruments may (a) require operators to provide access, (b) reduce the costs of connection, and (c) increase the number and types of suppliers.

Instruments Requiring Operators to Provide Access

Imposing connection obligations on an operator may require including service obligations in the contract and specifying connection targets.

SERVICE OBLIGATIONS. The most common way to introduce a commitment is by specifying universal service obligations (USOs). These provide a legal expression to the social objective of bringing infrastructure services to all households. Such objectives can also be justified in terms of the social benefits of universal coverage, such as reaping the full economies of scale from network expansion or securing positive externalities associated with access. The obligations can be defined in a variety of ways, and are often expressed in vague language. In the province of Santa Fe, Argentina, the water regulator has identified areas that require special treatment and specified the level of service to be delivered in these areas. In a typical formulation, the operator is required to provide the service to all households, or to all those that request the service. The obligation may be unidirectional, that is, incumbent only upon the operator, or bidirectional, meaning that the customer is also obliged to connect once the service has been made available (Chisari, Estache, and Romero 1999).

Unfortunately, because of their vagueness, USOs often raise as many questions as they answer (Chisari and Estache 1999). On its own, a USO may not be truly operational. Limitations in the coverage of the network may make fulfilling the obligation a physical impossibility in the short run. Even in communities already linked to the network, access charges may render a connection unaffordable, making the obligation irrelevant. These concerns highlight the need to complement a USO with requirements that specify the obligation in more detail and how the obligation is to be financed when customers lack the ability to pay.

Table 3.5. *Instruments for Promoting Access to Infrastructure Services*

Instrument	Advantages	Disadvantages
Imposing universal service obligations	Articulates the nature of social objectives toward the sector.	Requires complementary and coherent definitions of connection targets, access costs, and sources of subsidy funding to be operational.
Defining connection targets	Forces a concrete definition of realistic coverage targets. Can be monitored and enforced by use of financial penalties. Ensures that unprofitable customers are served.	Requires symmetrical obligation on users to connect, which limits freedom of choice. Attention must be given to affordability of connection charges if tariffs are to be met.
Using low-cost technologies	Offers consumer an appropriate balance between cost and quality.	May lead to reduced quality of service.
Providing credit for connections	Does not require external source of funding.	If provided by private operator, may increase risk exposure of operator. If not provided by operator, requires collaboration of microcredit institutions.
Cross-subsidizing connection costs	Does not require external source of funding and spreads cost over a large population (connected households have greater ability to pay than unconnected ones). Equitable if connections were provided free before privatization.	The unconnected population must be small relative to the connected population.

Subsidizing connections	Targets subsidy funds to low-income individuals. Administrative costs are relatively low as a proportion of subsidies awarded. For community-level subsidies, competitive forces can be used to keep costs down.	Requires government financing and is relatively costly per household connected. User cofinancing should be required to ensure commitment.
Obliging dominant utilities to provide alternative supplies	Ensures that a public alternative is available to households that are unable to connect to the network.	Except in the case of telephones, the evidence suggests that even poor households prefer private connections. Communal supply points tend to be unprofitable, and therefore need to be closely regulated.
Allowing licensed entry of alternative suppliers	Provides choice to consumers. Increases competitive pressure to the dominant utility.	May make investment unattractive to the dominant utility. May be difficult to regulate small suppliers to ensure adequate quality of service.
Promoting collaboration between dominant utility and alternative suppliers	May improve quality of supply to communities lacking connections to the dominant utility. May reduce commercial risk to dominant utility of serving marginal communities.	Requires careful regulation, as dominant utility may lack incentives to collaborate. Alternative suppliers may form local cartels.

Source: Authors.

CONNECTION TARGETS. Connection targets are a useful first step in clarifying the meaning of a USO for customer groups that are physically isolated from the network. Targets may also be necessary to ensure that coverage is provided to customer groups that are unprofitable to serve. Ideally, the targets specify the exact number of households, their geographic location, and the date by which they should be connected. Targets have the advantage of being easy to monitor, and can therefore be enforced by financial penalties. However, connection targets can only be met if customers take up the service, which will not always be the case. Households may be unwilling to connect to the sewerage network, for example, because they do not appreciate the wider social benefits. This type of argument is sometimes used to justify obligating customers to connect, which has the disadvantage of limiting customer choice. Furthermore, even when a customer wants to connect, the access charges may be unaffordable. Thus any serious attempt to increase coverage among poor households may require a serious assessment of connection charges.

Instruments Reducing Connection Costs

There are four main strategies for reducing connection costs, namely:

- Selecting cheaper technologies to reduce the costs associated with network expansion
- Spreading connection costs over time through the design of financing arrangements
- Cross-subsidizing between new and existing customers
- Using connection subsidies where public money is available.

CHEAPER TECHNOLOGIES. A common concern among the regulators of network industries is ensuring that costs are minimized. For many areas inhabited by the poor, the connection to a large network is not necessarily the least costly solution and is generally not the best solution, considering the short-run budget constraints of the poor. The preferred solution to ease access may often mean finding a combination of technology choice and quality of service that can allow faster and cheaper access for the poor. The key is to avoid prescribing single quality standards, specific technologies, or exclusivity rights to the main operator within the legal and regulatory framework instituted at the time of sector reform.

In Bolivia, for example, the private concessionaire in La Paz and El Alto was allowed to introduce a low-cost technology to make water and sewerage connections more affordable to low-income households, and it used volunteer community labor to install the system. As a result, the cost of installing water and sewerage systems each fell by about 40 percent. The total savings in connection charges are equivalent to 80 percent of households' monthly income of $122 in the poor neighborhoods. This approach helped to increase potable water and sewerage coverage in the poorest neighborhoods by about 20 percentage points. The company expects to have 100 percent water system coverage in El Alto by the end of 2001 (see box 3.3). In Chile, electricity and telecommunications operators are encouraged to find innovative ways to reduce the cost of bringing the services to rural communities (see box 3.4). This approach has more recently been extended to other countries in the region. As illustrated in table 3.6, Colombia, Guatemala, and Peru have all introduced similar programs for rural telephony. In combination, these four countries have brought telecommunications to some 9 million rural people. Moreover, each dollar of government subsidy has mobilized between $2 and $7 of private investment.

Any solution that recognizes that poor users are also potential providers of labor can lead to mutually beneficial arrangements between operators and consumers. The water sector in Argentina seems to be a laboratory of creative approaches to ease affordability without any type of cash transfer. In some neighborhoods the population provides the labor needed to work on connections or maintenance. Similar programs were implemented in the early 1990s in Mexico for road maintenance with impressive success rates. Such arrangements cut costs to the operators, have the potential to generate lasting employment, and clearly improve affordability.

FINANCING ARRANGEMENTS. Many low-income households lack the savings to pay connection costs up-front but may be able to afford the costs if they were spread across a number of installments. Because they pose a high credit risk and lack collateral, such households lack access to loans. A possible solution is to combine a network expansion program with a credit scheme. The two main options are to rely on the private operator to provide financing or to develop microfinancing options.

Relying on a private utility means having the operator go to the market and borrow to finance the expansion. Under such circumstances the operator must be granted the right to bill users for the amortization of the investment and the financing charges. Having the private operator act as credit provider has several advantages. First, the operator will have a lower cost of capital than low-income households, thereby reducing financing costs. Second, the operator can overcome the absence of collateral by using the threat of service disconnection to enforce loan repayment. This approach

---

Box 3.3. *Promoting Access to Water and Sanitation in El Alto, Bolivia*

In 1997 the government of Bolivia issued a 30-year concession to the Suez Lyonnaise des Eaux consortium (Aguas del Illimani) for private provision of water and sanitation services in the cities of La Paz and El Alto. A major objective of the concession was to increase coverage of these services rapidly, particularly in El Alto, a city adjacent to La Paz that was established in recent decades as a result of migration from mining centers and agricultural areas. At the time of the concession award, coverage was 87 percent for water and 48 percent for sewerage.

Reflecting this over-riding objective, the bidding for the connection was in terms of the number of new connections to be offered in return for a pre-determined water tariff. Specifically, the residential tariff was fixed at $0.22 per cubic meter following a 35 percent increase immediately before privatization. This tariff, which covers both water and sewerage services, is believed to represent about half of the true cost of provision. Industrial customers, who pay $0.66 to $1.18 per cubic meter, cover the difference. The winning bidder promised to achieve coverage close to 100 percent for water and 90 percent for sewerage in El Alto by 2001. The concession contract set connection charges at $155 for water and $188 for sewerage, which is thought to be below the full economic cost of $300 and $400, respectively, suggesting that a significant proportion of the costs of network expansion are probably being recovered via cross-subsidies from the use of service charge.

To make connection more affordable for low-income households, the concessionaire chose to expand the network in low-income areas applying "condominial" designs (which connect groups of households to the network rather than making an individual connection to each household) and using volunteer community labor to carry out the civil works. As a result, the cost of network expansion was reduced by about 40 percent for both the water and sewerage service with charges of $100 per connection. Following connection to water and sewerage networks, about 70 percent of households went on to build their own bathroom installations, some with the assistance of microcredit facilities. The total cost of this investment is typically around $500. Microcredit is provided at interest rates of around 14 percent for a five-year period.

Revenue recovery by the concessionaire has been as high as 98 percent, even in the low-income areas of El Alto, partly because of the introduction of convenient payment centers in the low-income areas. The main commercial problem for the concessionaire has been the low levels of demand, largely due to the lack of a local hygiene culture. Household consumption in El Alto is extremely low: 5 cubic meters per month for households with water but no sanitary installation, and only 10 cubic meters per month for households with full sanitary installations.

Source: Carbonel (2000); Foster (2001); Foster and Irusta (2001); Komives and Brook Cowen (1999).

Box 3.4. *Minimum Subsidy Concessions for Electricity and Telephones in Chile*

Chile has had successful experiences with minimum subsidy concessions to expand both electricity and public telephone services to rural communities since 1994. While the programs are separately administered, they share some common design features. Both programs make extensive use of competition at various stages. Competition exists between regional governments for central government financing, between rural communities for regional government sponsorship, and between utility companies for concessions to serve particular rural communities. Concessions are awarded to the company offering the largest reduction to the maximum allowable subsidy stipulated for each contract.

Service expansion is cofinanced by the state, the private sector, and rural consumers. State contributions are justified, because the projects identified have positive social returns, but negative private returns. Indeed, this differential defines the maximum allowable subsidy. However, the private operator finances a substantial part of the investment costs. The average proportion for telecommunications was 72 percent during 1995–97. For electricity, consumers are required to contribute the costs of the connection, the meter, and the in-house wiring, although this is typically spread over time. For both electricity and telephones, customers must pay regulated service charges to cover the unsubsidized costs.

Concessionaires are free to choose the appropriate technology. Although the government makes certain assumptions about technology choice in computing the maximum allowable subsidy, the winning bidder is free to select a technological solution. In electricity, for example, photovoltaic cells, microhydrolectric supply, and renewables may be used in addition to conventional grid extension.

The results of the programs have been encouraging. Coverage of electricity in rural areas increased from 53 to 76 percent during 1992–97, and the percentage of the population without access to a public telephone fell from 15 percent in 1994 to 1 percent by 1999. This progress was achieved at a cost of $1,100 per household for electricity and $2,300 per public telephone. Unit costs have risen for both services over the life of the programs, probably because later projects have been targeted toward more isolated communities that are more costly to serve.

Source: Jadresic (2000); Serra (2000).

Table 3.6. *Summary of Rural Telecommunications Programs, Chile, Colombia, Guatemala, and Peru*

Category	Chile	Colombia	Guatemala	Peru
Population served (millions)	2.2	3.7	1.6	1.3
Towns served (number)	6,059	7,415	4,420	1,598
Subsidy per town ($/town)	3,600	4,600	9,500	4,400
Percentage of estimated subsidy required (%)	60	45	37	78
Ratio of subsidy to private investment	1:7	—	1:2–3	1:2–4

— Not available.
Source: Izaguirre (2001).

has been adopted with some success in the Buenos Aires water concession (see box 3.5). Experience suggests that the main concern is that the amortization period must be consistent with an affordable monthly amortization bill—the longer the amortization period, the lower the monthly connection repayment. In Colombia, the law requires that connection charges for customers from lower socioeconomic groups be spread over at least three years.

While the operator may be a natural source of credit for connection costs, many households will also need loans to cover the costs of complementary installations within the household, such as wiring and plumbing. Here the case for the operator being involved in providing credit is not as clear, so alternative sources of finance must be sought. Microcredit schemes are a possible solution. These have been used with some success in Bolivia, although the evidence suggests that take-up is not concentrated among the poorest households. Microfinance may also provide a viable alternative to operator-based financing of connection costs, particularly if a high volume of loans to low-income customers would lead to significant increases in the operator's marginal cost of capital, thereby raising the overall cost of financing investments in the network.

CROSS-SUBSIDIZATION. Policymakers continue to be emotional, and sometimes dogmatic, when discussing subsidies. While in an ideal world the best subsidy is clearly the targeted lump sum cash payment, in most Latin American countries fiscal constraints impede the financing of many subsidies. In that context, cross-subsidies may be a reasonable option. The approach taken here is pragmatic and relies on evaluating the relative strengths and weaknesses of the feasible policy instruments available in any particular case.

Box 3.5. *Expanding Coverage of Water and Sanitation in Buenos Aires, Argentina*

In 1992 Suez-Lyonnaise des Eaux was awarded a 30-year concession contract to provide water and sanitation services in Greater Buenos Aires. The concessionaire won based on a promised tariff reduction of 27 percent, which was partially offset by a 13.5 percent tariff increase resulting from contract renegotiations in 1994. At the start of the concession, service coverage was 70 percent for water and 58 percent for sewerage. The coverage deficit was concentrated in the rapidly growing low-income suburbs, where only 55 percent of homes had a water connection and 36 percent had a sewerage connection. The concession incorporated connection targets designed to ensure that coverage rates reached 100 percent for water and 90 percent for sewerage by the end of the 30-year period.

Given the initial distribution of connections, six of every seven new connections were to be made among poor socioeconomic groups with monthly household income as low as $200 to $245. In comparison with these resources, the access charges in the contract were high. Depending on the characteristics of the property, the overall cost in 1995 ranged from $251 to $637 per household for water, and $856 to $891 for sewerage. These costs included an infrastructure charge for secondary network expansion apart from the connection fee. The concessionaire was required to allow customers to spread the infrastructure charge over a two-year period; however, this still represented an average cost of $44 per month, or a fifth of the income of a poor household.

The high level of the charges generated hostility from customers. This was exacerbated because connection, which had been free before the concession, was now mandatory and the alternative systems the households had been using were outlawed. Following some modest reductions to the charges in 1995, a crisis point was reached in 1997. After new negotiations, the infrastructure charge was abolished and replaced by a universal service and environmental improvement fee of $3 per month for all customers. Furthermore, the connection fee was reduced substantially to $120 for water, to be paid off in installments as low as $4 per month (see the following table). This amounted to a cross-subsidy between new and existing users. Because existing users were from better-off groups, the change did not provoke serious opposition.

(box continues on following page)

Box 3.5. *(continued)*

Monthly Water Bills for New and Existing Customers before and after Change ($)

Charges	Before	After
Existing customer		
Service charge	30.80	30.80
USEI fee	n.a.	6.00
Total charge (including value added tax)	37.26	44.52
New customer (water only)		
Service charge	6.16	6.16
Infrastructure charge	44.00	n.a.
USEI fee	n.a.	3.00
Connection charge	n.a.	4.00
Total charge (including value added tax)	60.69	15.92

n.a. Not applicable.
USEI Universal service and environmental improvement fee.
Source: Alcazar, Abdala, and Shirley (1999); Ferro (1999).

Cross-subsidies are normally discussed in the context of applying different user charges to different categories of customers. However, this approach may also be applied to make existing customers contribute part of the cost of expanding the system to reach new customers. There are a number of reasons to believe that this type of cross-subsidy may be much more reasonable and effective than the traditional sort that moves between different categories of users.

- As long as the size of the unconnected population is small relative to the size of the connected population, cross-subsidization spreads the costs of network expansion over a much larger number of households, and generally at a reasonably low cost to each household. The charge that each household pays to be connected is reduced and becomes sustainable economically and politically.
- Cross-subsidies toward new connections are in many cases more likely to reach the poor, because those lacking connections are predominantly poor.

- By reallocating a significant proportion of the cost to higher-income households (those who already have a connection), the private operator's payment risk can be reduced.
- Cross-subsidization circumvents the need for government funding, thereby retaining the sector's financial self-sufficiency.
- Cross-subsidization may be justified on ethical grounds if the richer groups of households that are already connected benefited from their connection at highly subsidized rates when the utility was still a public monopoly.

Even when existing customers receive their connections free of charge or at a rate heavily subsidized by the state, some arbitrariness is always involved in allocating costs between customers in a network industry. Arguably, the need for investments in network expansion has as much to do with the growth of demand from existing customers as with the arrival of new customers. Consequently, whether all these costs should be recovered by capital contributions from newly connected households, rather than by increases in the average tariff for all customers, is questionable. The water concession in Buenos Aires provides an example of how cross-subsidization was used to resolve a political crisis resulting from extremely high connection charges for new, often poor, customers (see box 3.5).

While cross-subsidization can work in a sector such as water and sewerage that has no competition for customers, it can also be adapted for use in competitive sectors such as telecommunications. To avoid cream-skimming or red-lining by new entrants, it is feasible to apply a uniform levy to the charges of all companies participating in the market. The government collects these universal service funds and reallocates them to those operators who connect new customers so as to meet the shortfall between the regulated connection charge and the economic costs of connection. This approach has been widely applied in the telecommunications sector.

CONNECTION SUBSIDIES. None of the preceding instruments require external financing from the government. When needed, direct subsidies for connection at the household or community levels are still an option. At the household level, governments may offer to cover a certain percentage of the connection costs, using socioeconomic criteria to identify the poor. The subsidy can be targeted to the specific component of the costs that may be most problematic for low-income households. One-time subsidies for capital costs are also administratively more cost-effective than recurring subsidies for the use of service (Foster, Gomez-Lobo, and Halpern 2000).

Direct connection subsidies to households are rare in Latin America, while community-level subsidies are more popular as a way to bring infrastructure services to rural areas, particularly in telecommunications. The idea is to grant a private operator a subsidy to provide loss-making services to a rural community. The approach was pioneered in Chile in 1994 to promote rural electrification and access to public telephones (see box 3.4). An attractive feature of this instrument is the possibility of using competitive tendering to find the private operator willing to provide the service at the lowest subsidy. This helps to contain the costs of increasing service coverage.

Instruments Increasing the Number and Types of Suppliers

Poor households often use alternative suppliers to meet their infrastructure needs when they do not have access to a conventional utility or when utility costs are too high (see Solo 1999a,b; Solo and Paniagua 1999). These suppliers offer a mixture of non-network (for example, tanker) services and private network services, or even hybrid systems in which local private networks receive water from a communal tank. In five major Latin American cities, alternative providers accounted for 15 to 50 percent of the market (see table 3.7). While non-network providers tend to be considerably more expensive than the conventional utilities, network providers are often able to undercut the dominant firm by using lower-cost and smaller-scale technologies (as in Asuncion, Barranquilla, Cordoba, and Guatemala City).

Table 3.7. *Market Shares and Unit Prices for Utilities and Alternative Providers, Selected Latin American Cities*

City and country	Share of the market (percent)		Average tariff ($/m³)	
	Conventional utility	Independent providers	Conventional utility	Independent providers
Asuncion, Paraguay	70	30	0.40	0.30–0.40
Barranquilla, Colombia	75	20	0.55	0.54–6.40
Cordoba, Argentina	75	15	0.54	0.27–2.00
Guatemala City, Guatemala	50	50	0.09–0.42	0.25–2.70
Lima, Peru	74	26	0.29	0.29–2.43

Source: Solo (1999b).

The evidence suggests that alternative network providers compete among each other, particularly along boundary areas between suppliers. Alternative suppliers achieve high revenue recovery rates compared with public utilities, often because they know their customers personally. As substitutes for a conventional household connection can play a fundamental role in meeting basic needs, policies to promote access should not overlook the role alternative network and non-network supplies can play. Considering the entire market for services is essential to ensure that the reform process benefits poorer households that lack a conventional private connection. Various instruments are available for considering alternative suppliers. They range from mandating the dominant utility to provide substitute services, to providing a legitimate role for alternative suppliers, to promoting cooperation between the dominant utility and alternative suppliers.

Conventional utilities are often constrained in the technology they use, namely, the network connection. In some cases, it may make sense to redefine the utility's obligation in terms of providing a *service* (such as water, sanitation, or lighting) by whatever technological means are deemed appropriate, rather than providing a specific type of network *connection*. The utility is then responsible for making the service available to all customers, including those served by communal supply points or non-network substitutes. For example, a water utility could distribute water via tanker service. A potential disadvantage of this approach is that it may limit competition in the provision of non-network-based services that are not naturally monopolistic. However, even without a legal monopoly, the dominant utility may engage in unfair competition with non-network suppliers by practicing cross-subsidies between network and non-network customers, or by restricting competitors' access to bulk supply from its network.

These problems can, in principle, be avoided by regulatory means, but the best approach is to avoid a market structure likely to generate difficulties. Competition is less of an issue for communal supply points—street lighting, public standpipes, public toilets, or public telephones—because public facilities are often loss-making activities, so no competitors exist. In such circumstances specifying contractual obligations such as installing loss-making public telephones in rural areas may be necessary (Melo 2000). Only in rare cases can community supply points be provided competitively by non-network means. In Peru, microentrepreneurs operate mobile public telephones using cellular technology. They wear brightly colored hats and clothing to attract attention and have earned the nickname *cholos celulares* (cellular Indians) (Melo 2000).

The legalization and licensing of alternative suppliers may help subject the dominant utility to competitive pressure. Full liberalization generates the highest competitive pressures, but some argue that in the water sector private operators require service area exclusivity to take the risk of investing in network expansions. As to whether alternative suppliers should be regulated, most regulatory frameworks ignore alternative suppliers, and if non-network services are truly competitive, price regulation should not be necessary. However, anecdotal evidence suggests that alternative suppliers do not always operate competitively, for example, by forming local cartels. Such problems are often exacerbated by illegality, and in these cases legalization may help to promote competition.

Even where genuine competition exists, regulation of quality can still be an issue, because consumers may not be in a position to assess the safety of water or power supplies until it is too late. The burden of monitoring quality among a wide array of small suppliers is potentially large, but may be reduced by forming associations and forging partnerships between alternative suppliers and the dominant utility. Another approach is to bid out short horizon concessions for truck-based retailing of water and sanitation services in specific neighborhoods, similar to what is often done for garbage collection. If problems occur, the concessions can then be revoked.

In some cases the most efficient solution may be to require collaboration between the dominant utility and alternative suppliers. For example, the dominant utility may have a comparative advantage in producing a resource such as clean water or electricity, perhaps because of economies of scale or limited availability of water sources, while the alternative supplier may have a comparative advantage in distribution and retailing. The alternative supplier may also have greater flexibility to use a technology more closely matched to the needs of the local community, and may be willing to take on the commercial risk of billing marginal neighborhoods where local knowledge may enable higher rates of revenue collection. The promotion of partnerships requires appropriate design of the regulatory framework, because the legal framework would need to allow intermediaries to act as secondary retailers of utility services in the residential market. The regulations also need to clarify the nature of bulk supply arrangements between the dominant utility and secondary retailers, for example, by specifying how the price and availability of bulk supplies will be determined. Again, a critical question is the extent to which secondary retailers should be subject to price and quality regulation.

Concluding Comments

The good news is that access rates are improving, and as access improves the poor tend to benefit. The bad news is that growth rates are slow, and if the current trends continue, supplying access to safe water to more than 90 percent of the population may take another 20 years. Mitigating policy actions can be taken, however, to speed up the process, or at least to accelerate access among the poor. Whether they consist of mandating that operators provide access, easing the choice among suppliers, or reducing the costs of connection, the choices will have to be tailored to the specific needs of each sector in each country. In some of the poorest countries or regions, these measures alone will probably not be enough to help the poor. Help will also be needed in making sure that consumption is affordable.

Appendix 3.1. Access to Electricity, Water, and Telephone, by Country, Selected Years, 1986–96

Country and year	Percentage of households with access											Per capita GDP (1995 $)	Survey expanded sample size (millions)	Survey population coverage (percent)
	National			Urban			Rural							
	Electricity	Water	Phone	Electricity	Water	Phone	Electricity	Water	Phone					
Argentina														
1986	n.a.	n.a.	n.a.	99.70	97.05	n.a.	n.a.	n.a.	n.a.			7,473.25	10.40	33.81
1989	n.a.	n.a.	n.a.	99.54	95.79	n.a.	n.a.	n.a.	n.a.			6,707.39	11.09	34.55
1992	n.a.	n.a.	n.a.	99.96	97.16	n.a.	n.a.	n.a.	n.a.			7,670.21	11.66	34.91
1995	n.a.	n.a.	n.a.	99.78	96.94	n.a.	n.a.	n.a.	n.a.			8,075.78	11.44	32.89
1996	n.a.	n.a.	n.a.	99.86	98.17	n.a.	n.a.	n.a.	n.a.			8,353.19	11.56	32.83
Bolivia														
1986	n.a.	n.a.	n.a.	97.27	76.08	n.a.	n.a.	n.a.	n.a.			797.37	2.07	34.39
1989	n.a.	n.a.	n.a.	90.30	70.92	n.a.	n.a.	n.a.	n.a.			817.41	2.44	37.97
1992	n.a.	n.a.	n.a.	90.60	75.79	n.a.	n.a.	n.a.	n.a.			852.27	2.45	35.55
1996	66.54	60.47	n.a.	93.92	83.39	n.a.	25.00	25.69	n.a.			921.25	4.57	60.28
Brazil														
1986	81.13	67.74	n.a.	95.84	82.81	n.a.	41.71	27.34	n.a.			4,278.45	135.61	98.31
1989	85.10	70.77	n.a.	96.85	83.62	n.a.	51.17	33.67	n.a.			4,333.06	144.06	98.95
1995	90.65	78.28	20.51	98.38	88.60	25.09	61.60	39.50	3.30			4,417.51	152.37	95.70
1996	91.93	81.59	23.58	98.72	91.26	28.64	67.24	46.45	5.17			4,480.27	154.36	95.66
Chile														
1992	87.69	86.10	n.a.	94.28	97.53	n.a.	59.09	36.47	n.a.			3,502.12	13.45	97.96
1998	96.82	90.19	14.27	99.58	99.25	16.37	80.65	37.09	1.97			4,419.24	14.49	100.52

Colombia												
1989	n.a.	n.a.	n.a.	99.32	97.29	62.38	n.a.	n.a.	n.a.	2,071.61	10.92	33.05
1992	n.a.	n.a.	n.a.	99.48	97.51	64.04	n.a.	n.a.	n.a.	2,161.87	12.46	35.74
1995	94.56	84.23	39.46	99.74	97.77	62.32	87.20	64.96	6.93	2,407.19	20.22	54.92
1996	91.70	81.68	39.86	98.92	97.90	60.42	80.61	56.76	8.30	2,410.15	23.38	62.44
El Salvador												
1989	n.a.	n.a.	n.a.	89.71	58.76	12.22	n.a.	n.a.	n.a.	n.a.	2.26	43.46
1992	n.a.	n.a.	n.a.	92.75	60.73	12.61	n.a.	n.a.	n.a.	n.a.	2.37	43.94
1995	74.34	44.46	14.08	94.69	66.92	25.41	49.78	17.36	0.41	n.a.	3.17	54.89
1996	75.65	47.80	16.66	94.89	69.21	30.11	52.40	21.91	0.40	n.a.	3.17	54.63
Guatemala												
1987	n.a.	n.a.	n.a.	n.a.	n.a.	n.a.	n.a.	n.a.	n.a.	n.a.	8.04	98.04
1989	50.09	53.08	n.a.	88.03	80.01	n.a.	27.69	37.18	n.a.	n.a.	5.83	65.21
1999	61.21	61.17	n.a.	90.27	88.83	n.a.	42.29	43.17	n.a.	n.a.	10.50	94.78
Honduras												
1986	50.73	75.81	n.a.	82.06	88.52	n.a.	n.a.	n.a.	n.a.	663.26	1.35	29.70
1989	41.57	66.55	n.a.	89.64	88.57	n.a.	18.34	55.91	n.a.	700.11	4.47	90.20
1992	55.47	87.04	n.a.	88.42	92.52	n.a.	31.58	83.07	n.a.	699.08	4.97	91.70
1995	53.31	n.a.	n.a.	86.22	n.a.	n.a.	28.10	n.a.	n.a.	698.29	5.33	91.80
1996	59.31	87.34	n.a.	94.84	96.74	n.a.	31.66	80.03	n.a.	703.56	5.55	91.00
Mexico												
1984	87.27	79.33	15.82	95.17	89.05	23.41	73.67	62.59	2.75	3,758.39	75.97	104.00
1989	89.15	78.10	18.22	97.23	90.92	27.90	76.14	57.46	2.63	3,924.34	78.74	96.30
1992	91.28	77.51	21.50	97.24	88.03	29.45	75.45	49.57	0.38	4,212.81	84.05	96.90
1994	93.49	79.57	25.80	97.59	89.57	35.16	82.43	52.63	0.60	4,323.41	89.37	99.30
1996	93.11	83.09	26.51	97.50	92.11	35.72	81.45	59.10	2.02	4,117.98	92.59	99.40

(appendix continues on following page)

53

Appendix 3.1. (continued)

Country and year	National Electricity	National Water	National Phone	Urban Electricity	Urban Water	Urban Phone	Rural Electricity	Rural Water	Rural Phone	Per capita GDP (1995 $)	Survey expanded sample size (millions)	Survey population coverage (percent)
Paraguay												
1986	n.a.	n.a.	n.a.	94.70	70.41	n.a.	n.a.	n.a.	n.a.	1,700.09	0.98	25.90
1989	n.a.	n.a.	n.a.	97.79	74.33	n.a.	n.a.	n.a.	n.a.	1,816.38	1.12	27.10
1992	n.a.	n.a.	n.a.	97.86	68.31	n.a.	n.a.	n.a.	n.a.	1,787.37	1.23	27.70
1995	n.a.	n.a.	n.a.	96.35	67.63	20.64	n.a.	n.a.	n.a.	1,860.45	1.41	29.20
1996	n.a.	n.a.	n.a.	96.94	67.14	n.a.	n.a.	n.a.	n.a.	1,835.77	1.49	30.20
Uruguay												
1981	n.a.	n.a.	n.a.	93.22	87.81	n.a.	n.a.	n.a.	n.a.	5,266.75	2.66	88.00
1989	n.a.	n.a.	n.a.	96.66	91.56	n.a.	n.a.	n.a.	n.a.	4,851.37	2.75	89.30
1992	n.a.	n.a.	n.a.	98.28	97.95	n.a.	n.a.	n.a.	n.a.	5,326.34	2.80	89.50
1995	n.a.	n.a.	n.a.	98.78	97.91	n.a.	n.a.	n.a.	n.a.	5,606.86	2.87	90.20
1996	n.a.	n.a.	n.a.	99.22	98.32	n.a.	n.a.	n.a.	n.a.	5,859.80	2.89	90.30
Republica Bolivariana de Venezuela												
1986	95.18	90.62	n.a.	99.35	96.96	n.a.	78.65	65.54	n.a.	3,496.11	17.90	101.70
1989	97.08	91.54	n.a.	99.50	96.61	n.a.	84.65	65.55	n.a.	3,245.65	19.38	101.80
1992	97.89	93.09	n.a.	99.58	97.64	n.a.	88.73	68.54	n.a.	3,725.42	20.35	99.60
1995	99.47	92.99	n.a.	99.57	97.69	n.a.	95.06	71.33	n.a.	3,537.19	21.85	100.00
1996	98.47	92.14	n.a.	99.53	97.00	n.a.	94.12	72.33	n.a.	3,449.36	22.32	100.00

Source: Authors; see also Wodon and Ajwad (2000a).

Appendix 3.2. Sector-Specific Access Rates by Income Deciles for Latin America, 1986–96

Electricity Access by Income Decile (National)

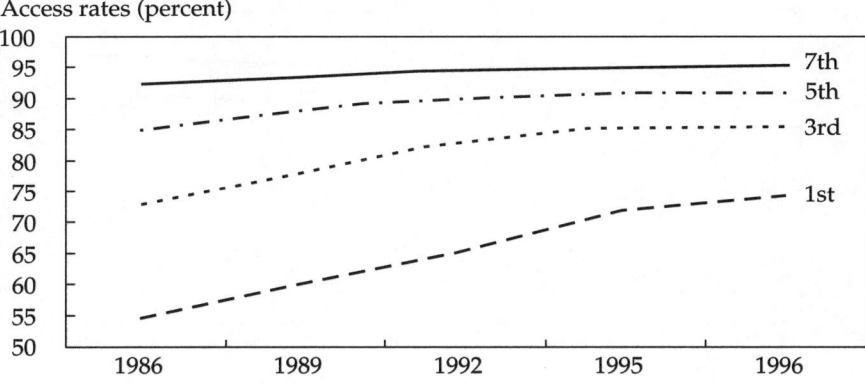

Electricity Access by Income Decile (Urban)

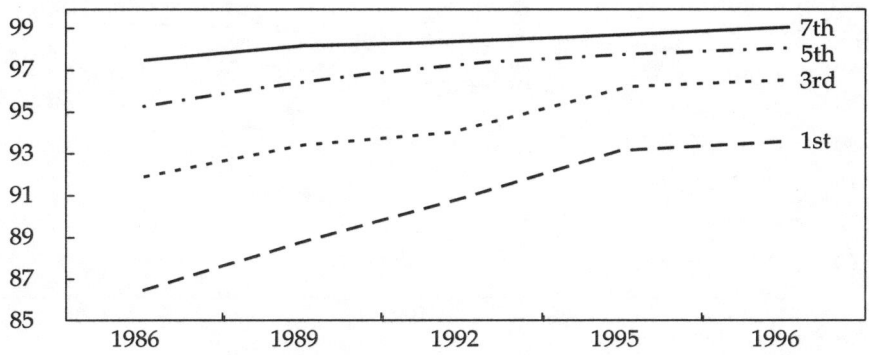

Electricity Access by Income Decile (Rural)

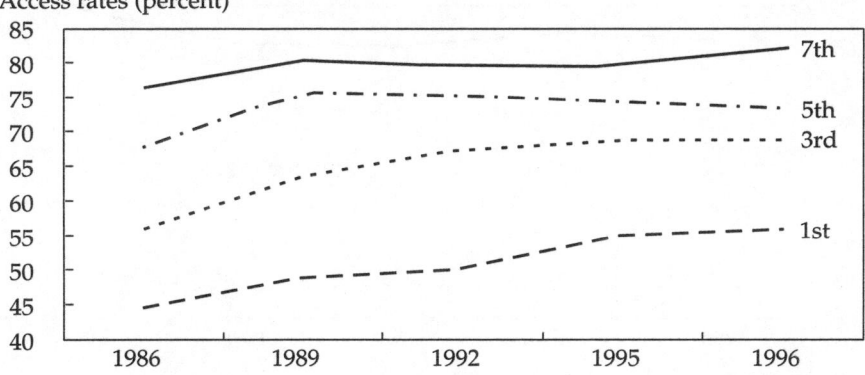

(appendix continues on following page)

Appendix 3.2. (continued)

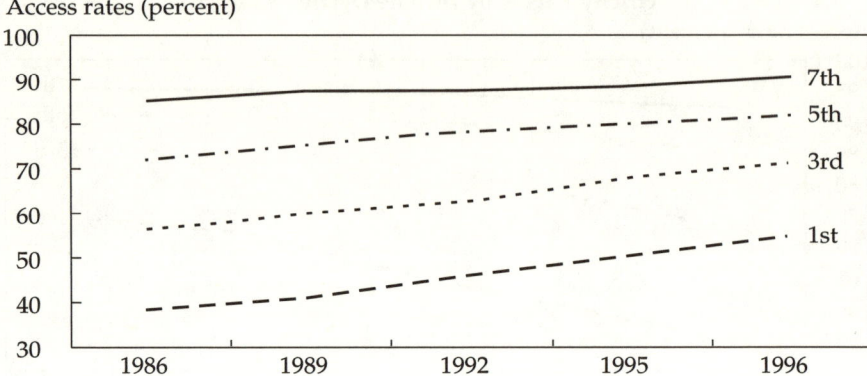

Water Access by Income Decile (National)

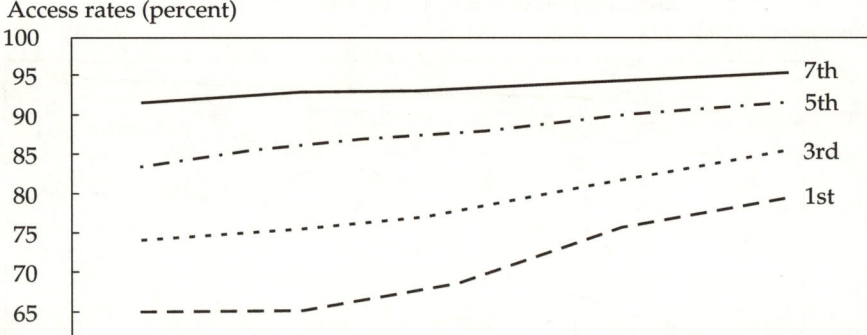

Water Access by Income Decile (Urban)

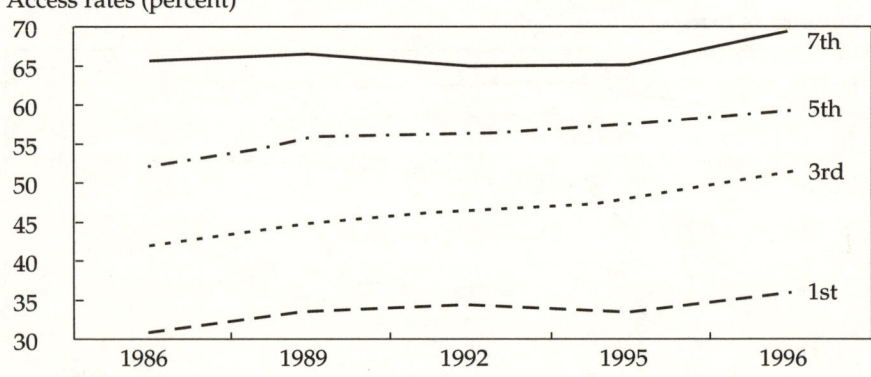

Water Access by Income Decile (Rural)

Source: Authors; see also Wodon and Ajwad (2000a).

4

Ensuring Consumption Affordability

Some policymakers argue that reform and increased private sector participation drive up prices and reduce affordability, making them reluctant to
consider this option. This chapter looks at the impact of reforms on consumption affordability and shows that the evidence is mixed. This is a challenge as we cannot provide price trends, because tariff structures are often
complex and can vary from one area to another or from one operator to
another within a country. Most household surveys also lack information
on prices for infrastructure services. Tracing changes in real prices for services since the mid-1980s in Latin America would be a valuable endeavor,
but is beyond the scope of this study. We have, however, been able to collect sufficient anecdotal evidence to draw some preliminary conclusions.
These suggest that while in some cases tariffs increase to reflect costs and
ensure that the operators have the incentive to continue maintaining infrastructure and investing as needed, in many other instances tariffs decrease
with private operation, particularly where competition can be introduced.

This chapter also illustrates that even when tariff increases are needed,
the government can chose mitigating instruments to reduce the burden on
the poor. Various subsidy, credit, or financing schemes can be introduced
in addition to cost-reduction strategies to help ensure that infrastructure
services are affordable to the poorest.

Impact of Infrastructure Reform

Reform generally results from a failure of the public operator to generate
enough revenue on its own to pay not only for new investment, but often
also to cover operational costs. One of the main conditions for private
participation is the guarantee that total revenue will cover total costs,

including the cost of capital. This may seem to imply that tariffs will increase and that the poor will suffer; however, this is not always so. When politicians keep the costs of operating the services artificially high—most notably by relying on public utilities as employment sources or by allowing corrupt procurement practices to inflate other costs—reform and private operation can result in lower costs and tariffs.

While prices do sometimes increase following infrastructure reform, some of the most publicized reforms—such as in Argentina and Chile, and in Bolivia and Colombia to a lesser extent—show that price reductions are not exceptions.

- *Water in Argentina.* In 1992 water and sanitation services in the Buenos Aires Metropolitan Region were concessioned for 30 years. The investment commitments were $4 billion for the period of the concession, and the contract was awarded to the company that offered the lowest tariff. Consequently, tariffs were reduced, on average, by 27 percent. A few years into the concession, renegotiation resulted in a tariff increase of 13.5 percent because of the need to bring advance investment plans and increase service quality. However, the net impact on prices was lower tariffs compared with the situation before services had been concessioned. This benefited all clients, including the poor, and illustrates how a well-designed bidding mechanism can lead to a significant tariff reduction for customers.
- *Electricity in Argentina.* The wholesale price of electricity dropped from $48.76 per megawatt hour in 1992 to $25.67 per megawatt hour in 1997, a drop of almost 50 percent during the five years following privatization. This decrease occurred as a result of competition leading to new entry in the generation sector; the number of generators increased from 13 in 1992 to 44 in 1997. The average retail price for residential customers (net of taxes) dropped by 40 percent, from an average of $0.191 per kilowatt (at constant 1997 prices) before 1991 to $0.115 per kilowatt in the five years after privatization. Although part of this 40 percent drop would probably have occurred without privatization, the magnitude of the price reduction strongly suggests that privatization is not always accompanied by tariff increases (Estache and Rodriguez-Pardina 2000, FIEL 2000). Competition appears to be key to keeping privatization from leading to increases in prices.
- *Telecommunications in Argentina.* Unlike the water and electricity sectors, the telecommunications sector saw significant increases in prices following privatization, largely because of the need to rebalance local

and long-distance charges. Between January and November 1990, during the buildup to privatization, the price of the basic "pulse" increased from $0.47 to $3.81. Since then, however, call prices have risen by significantly less than the rate of inflation (Abeles 2000).

- *Electricity and telecommunications in Chile.* When the long-distance market for telecommunications in Chile was liberalized in 1994, call prices dropped by more than 50 percent, and up to 80 percent for large clients. A similar drop in prices occurred in 1998 in the mobile telephony industry, following the award of licenses to use PCS technology, when the number of mobile telephone companies increased from two to four. In the electricity sector, generating prices fell by 50 percent between 1988 and 1998, primarily because of the arrival of natural gas from Argentina to fuel new combined cycle power plants. However, the privatization of the generation industry probably helped finance the gas pipeline. Retail electricity tariffs have not fallen by the same magnitude as generating prices, but fell by 25 percent between 1988 and 1998, again probably at least in part as a result of competition (Serra 2000).
- *Electricity in Bolivia.* While residential customers may have been less protected than industrial customers from the impact on prices of the electricity sector privatization, electricity customers still benefited from small price reductions after the reform (Ajwad, Anguizola, and Wodon 2000).
- *Electricity in Colombia.* A reform that rebalanced the tariff structure between fixed and variables charges and introduced a tariff differentiation by payment methods resulted in a rising block tariff structure. This allowed a redistribution of income from the rich to the poor (Maddock and Castano 1991).

The main point to be drawn from this limited survey is that discussions of the impact of reform and privatization in infrastructure are driven by many myths, and one of the most enduring is that they inevitably lead to price increases that hurt the poor. Enough examples exist to show that success stories are not exceptions and that win-win solutions are possible.

Improving Consumption Affordability for the Poorest

Success in achieving affordability is not random and requires conscious policy choices. Table 4.1 provides an inventory of the instruments that can be used to improve affordability and a brief overview of their advantages

Table 4.1. *Selected Instruments for Promoting Affordability of Infrastructure Services*

Instrument	Advantages	Disadvantages
Lifeline subsidies set by consumption level	Minimal administrative costs. Provides an incentive for large consumers to economize on use.	Poor customers are not necessarily small consumers, and lifeline or subsistence blocks are often set too high. Detrimental to coping strategies such as secondary retailing (purchasing agreements among the poor).
Means-tested subsidies set by customer group	Provides a more reliable way of identifying low-income households.	Difficulty of finding good targeting variables. Administrative costs may be significant. Difficulty of raising subsidy or cross-subsidy funds.
Means-tested vouchers for purchasing services	Same advantages as means-tested tariffs, with added flexibility for user to select service provider.	Same difficulties as means-tested tariffs, and need to establish funding mechanism to provide flexibility for beneficiaries to select their service provider.
Reduced standing versus usage charges	Reduces burden of fixed costs on small consumers.	The overall impact on affordability may not be large.
Controlling the level of consumption (service limiters and others)	Prevents low-income households from consuming beyond their means.	May lead to hardship if basic needs exceed imposed consumption ceiling. May not be technologically feasible (or technology may be costly). Runs against the private operator's commercial incentives.
Increasing the frequency of billing	Facilitates budgeting for low-income households.	Increases administrative costs of revenue collection, but may reduce collection costs.
Using prepayment devices	Facilitates budgeting for low-income households.	May lead to "self-disconnection." May be costly and subject to fraud. Requires the creation of a network for selling "smart cards" if electronic technology is used.

Source: Authors.

and disadvantages. These instruments influence affordability in at least one of three ways, namely,

- By reducing the bill to poor households
- By reducing the cost of services
- By facilitating the payment of bills.

Table 4.1 lists options that can be considered for any type of infrastructure reform. These should not be regarded as mutually exclusive, and successful examples from Latin America combine several of these instruments. Moreover, when the government finances any of these options and the infrastructure reform covers several sectors, coordinating implementation and assessing the burden on the treasury are important.

Three broad categories of instruments can soften the poor household's burden imposed by utility bills: targeting subsidies, rebalancing the tariff, and providing vouchers. The first two are common in Latin America; the third is not, but deserves consideration.

Targeted Subsidies

Targeting subsidies is the standard textbook recommendation to deal with the needs of the poor. Two broad approaches are available for targeting subsidies in infrastructure. First, they can be based on the consumption level of the households, in which case they are called "lifeline subsidies," or second, they can be based on socioeconomic characteristics, in which case they are referred to as means-tested subsidies. Both types are quite common under varying guises that reflect the creativity of policymakers in dealing with specific constraints in implementing targeted subsidies. In general, these subsidies face two main types of challenges: acquiring sufficient financing capacity and targeting resources effectively toward the poor. Enforcement requires information about the poor and their needs, and requires ensuring that the subsidy goes where intended and that the risks of leakage or fraud are minimized.

The most common approach to subsidizing tariffs to improve affordability for the poor is differentiating tariffs according to the volume of consumption. This provides an easy quantitative target as to what and how much to subsidize. One approach is the rising block tariff structure, with a low rate charged for an initial "lifeline" block of consumption, and progressively higher rates for successive blocks thereafter. An alternative is a subsidy whose amount depends negatively on total consumption, under the assumption that the poor tend to consume less than the rich. In Honduras the unit charge is reduced for customers with total consumption below 300 kilowatt hours a month. A common problem with these types of tariff structures in Latin America is that the lifeline block is relatively high compared with true subsistence needs. In La Paz, Bolivia, for example, the lifeline threshold for water is 30 cubic meters per month, even though average consumption is 5 cubic meters per month among poor households and 23 cubic meters per month among richer households.

One variation on this theme, common in the water and electricity sectors in Latin America, is to include a free initial block of consumption in the fixed charge. Although this does not provide customers with an incentive to keep consumption below the level of the initial block, it can help promote affordability. In Panama the water utility has a minimum charge of $6.40 per month, which entitles the consumer to 8,000 gallons of water per month. In Honduras the amount the electricity utility charges is fixed for consumption below 20 kilowatt hours per month.

Both approaches yield similar results, are easy to implement, with low administrative costs. However, they tend to be badly targeted, because consumption is only weakly correlated with income and poverty (Boland and Whittington 2000). Figure 4.1 illustrates this for water using data for Central

Figure 4.1. *Water Consumption by Quintile, Selected Central American Cities*

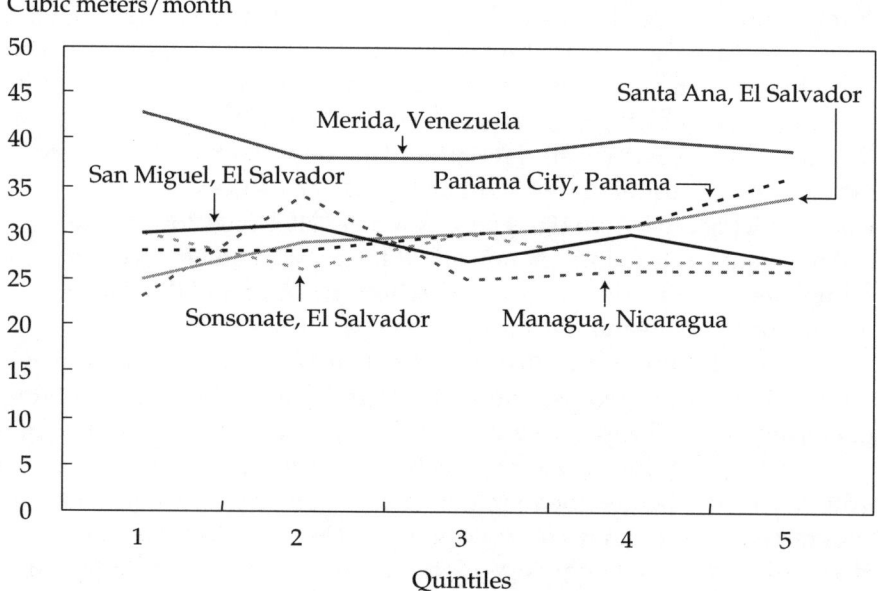

Source: Walker and others (2000).

Figure 4.2. *Electricity Consumption by Decile, Guatemala and Honduras*

Kilowatt hours/month

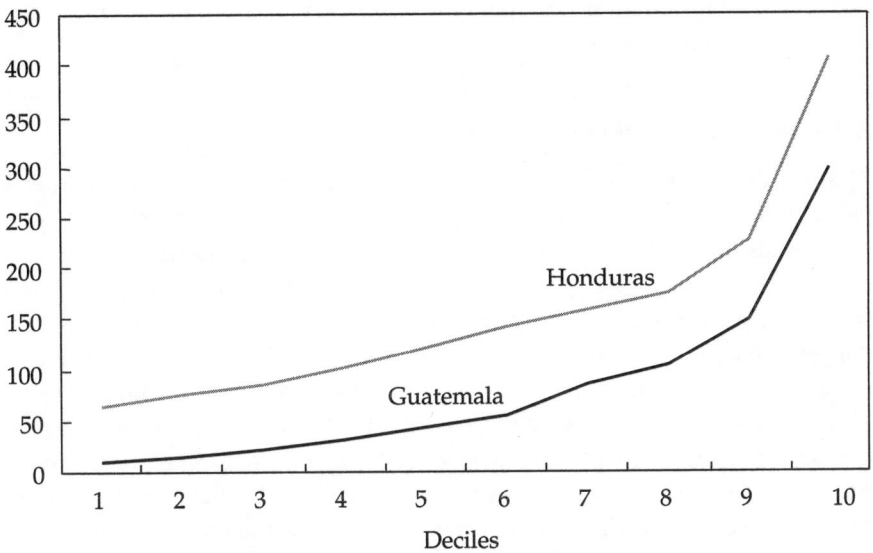

Deciles

Source: Authors' estimation based on national household surveys.

American cities. In figure 4.2, which shows electricity consumption in Guatemala and Honduras, the correlation between consumption and income is larger. Lifeline subsidies may still involve large errors of inclusion (see box 4.1), either because the consumption ceiling to benefit from the subsidy is set too high (as in Honduras), or because those connected to the grid tend to be relatively well off, because the poorest do not typically have an electricity connection. Furthermore, even when poor households are connected to the grid, they will not necessarily register very low levels of consumption. This is true for a variety of reasons, including the large size of poor households, sheltering agreements among the poor (two households in one dwelling), and purchasing agreements between neighbors, all of which lead to relatively high levels of consumption from a single connection. Thus understanding the prevalence of these types of living arrangements in any particular city or country is extremely important when designing tariff structures.

Under means-tested subsidies, households' eligibility is based on observable characteristics of the household or its dwelling, under the assumption that these characteristics are correlated with income, and therefore with poverty. In Chile households must undergo a socioeconomic interview before they can be declared eligible for subsidized water tariffs. In Colombia all utility tariffs are differentiated according to the characteristics of the property and its surrounding neighborhood. Box 4.2 summarizes the experience of these countries.

Rebalancing Fixed and Variable Tariffs

Many utility tariff structures include a combination of fixed and variable charges. Fixed charges such as standing charges for water and electricity or line rentals for telecommunications are paid irrespective of the level of consumption. Variable charges reflect the amount of the service used. High fixed charges will make services unattractive to small consumers. The burden of fixed charges falls disproportionately on households with low levels of consumption, which may also often be low-income households. Traditional substitute services (for example, tanker water or candles) do not typically include fixed charges, and so may be financially more attractive to small consumers even though the variable charges may be higher. For any level of the standing charge, a break-even level of consumption exists below which using traditional substitutes is cheaper, as shown in figure 4.3).

One option for rebalancing is to keep fixed charges low for all customers and recover almost all costs through the variable charge. A second possibility is to offer a menu of tariffs with different combinations of standing and variable charges, leaving customers to select the tariff structure that they find most attractive. A third possibility is to keep a common variable charge for all customers, but to allow the fixed charge to vary according with the socioeconomic characteristics of a household.

The conclusion is that to be able to design tariff structures that are sensitive to the needs of the poor, policymakers must have information about the consumption levels of rich and poor households. Such data are not readily available; however, in many cases they may be derived from household surveys that collect information about expenditure on utility services.

Vouchers

Although voucher programs have not been implemented in Latin America, they have been in existence for energy consumption in the United States since 1980. President Carter created the energy voucher program (Low

Box 4.1. *Targeting Subsidies According to Consumption Level (Lifeline Subsidies)*

In Honduras, the national electric utility receives a government subsidy to reduce the cost of electricity for all households consuming less than 300 kilowatt hours per month. The total cost of the subsidy in 2000 was about $17 million. Wodon, Ajwad, and Siaens (2000) show that the subsidy is not effective at reducing poverty, because most of it is spent on households that consume 100 to 300 kilowatt hours per month, and these households tend to have a relatively low probability of being poor. The table below shows the current structure of electricity consumption by level, together with the existing subsidy. For example, the share of connected households with monthly consumption less than 20 kilowatt hours is 20.31 percent (115,723 households), of which 44.93 percent are poor. With average consumption of 3.36 kilowatt hours per household per month, the total consumption for this group is 388,626 kilowatt hours per month. Without the subsidy, this group would have to pay a total bill of L 929,256, but this is reduced to L 303,282 when the subsidy of L 595,973 is taken into account ($1 = L 17).

Targeting Performance of Honduras's Subsidy among Connected Households

Consumption level (kwh)	Share of clients (%) (1)	Share of clients in poverty (%) (2)	Error of inclusion (%) (1)*[1–(2)]	Error of exclusion (%) (1)*(2)	Average consumption (kwh)	Total bill without subsidy (L)	Total subsidy (L)	Share of subsidy spent on nonpoor households (%)
0–20	20.31	44.93	11.18	n.a.	3.36	929,256	595,973	1.38
20–100	22.69	35.66	14.60	n.a.	58.67	5,095,693	2,716,580	7.30
100–150	12.63	16.82	10.50	n.a.	125.09	7,387,370	3,761,883	13.14
150–200	11.16	10.98	9.94	n.a.	175.35	10,314,338	5,148,710	19.24
200–250	9.25	15.64	7.81	n.a.	224.54	11,618,468	5,746,445	20.35
250–300	7.43	17.09	6.16	n.a.	275.77	11,895,559	5,850,730	20.36
300+	16.53	10.15	n.a.	9.22	n.a.	n.a.	n.a.	n.a.
Total	100.00	24.96	60.19	9.22	108.58	47,240,684	23,820,321	81.81

n.a. Not applicable.
kwh Kilowatt hour.
Source: Wodon, Ajwad, and Siaens (2000).

(box continues on following page)

Box 4.1. *(continued)*

To measure the targeting performance of the subsidy among the population with a connection to the electricity grid, summary statistics can be used.
Denote by SP and SP_k the shares of the poor among, respectively, all customers and the customers in consumption interval k, by S_k the share of all customers in interval k, and by M the consumption threshold for subsidy
eligibility.

- *Errors of inclusion (E1) and exclusion (E2):* E1 is the share of the nonpoor
  benefiting from the subsidy: $E1 = \Sigma_{k \leq M} S_k(1 - SP_k)/(1 - SP)$. E2 is the
  share of the poor not benefiting from the subsidy: $E2 = \Sigma_{k > M} S_k SP_k / SP$.
  As *E1* increases, *E2* decreases, and vice versa. The error of inclusion
  E1 is 60.19 percent, and the error of exclusion *E2* is 9.22 percent.
- *Ratio of poor versus nonpoor beneficiaries:* This is equal to $(1 - E2)*SP/$
  $[E1*(1 - SP)]$. With $SP = 0.2496$, the ratio is 0.5072 percent, so that the
  number of nonpoor households receiving the subsidy is about twice
  as large as the number of the poor receiving the subsidy.
- *Share of subsidies given to the nonpoor:* This share depends on the distribution of the subsidies. It is above 80 percent, which implies that the
  impact on poverty of the electricity subsidy is small in comparison to
  the public cost.

Source: Wodon, Ajwad, and Siaens (2000).

Income Home Energy Assistance Program) to help the poor pay for their
energy needs following rising energy prices. The program has three main
components: (a) a crisis component for preventing utility disconnection in
times of extremely hot or cold weather, (b) a year-round heating and cool-
ing assistance component, and (c) a weatherization component to improve
home energy efficiency. The program works through block grants that are
awarded annually to the 50 U.S. states and the District of Columbia, to
Indian tribes and tribal organizations, and to isolated areas to help low-
income households meet their home energy costs. Each state can specify
different targeting and allocation criteria, if they follow a few federal guidelines (Wodon 2000c). The program must rely on some form of means-testing,
thus its strengths and weaknesses are broadly similar to those of means-
tested subsidies.

Box 4.2. *Targeting Subsidies According to Socioeconomic Status (Means-Tested Subsidies)*

In Chile, to attenuate the impact on the poor of rising prices after the reform of the water sector in 1990, the government introduced a subsidy to ensure that no household would spend more than 5 percent of its income on water and sewerage. Initial take-up of the program was low, at only 5 percent of potential beneficiaries, probably because both the eligibility threshold and the value of the subsidy were too low to give households much of an incentive to apply. Following a series of modifications, including allowing water companies to propose customers as potential subsidy recipients, take-up rates increased to 42 percent by 1991, 85 percent by 1994, and 95 percent by 1997.

Today the system offers a subsidy of 20 to 85 percent of the household water bill for the first 15 cubic meters of monthly consumption. Using regional data on water consumption and tariffs, as well as socioeconomic conditions, the Ministry of Planning determines the total funds made available to each region. Within each region, subsidies are allocated to municipalities that determine household eligibility using a standardized socioeconomic scoring system (CAS). Water companies can apply for the subsidy on behalf of their customers. Eligibility is reassessed every three years, and the subsidy can be withdrawn if households are more than three months in arrears with their water bills.

Colombia has applied subsidies for utility services since the 1960s, using the characteristics of the dwelling and its immediate neighborhood as proxies for income in a six-tier classification of households. Households from the lower-income strata are eligible for a percentage reduction in their water and energy bills. This subsidy is financed by applying a percentage surcharge on the bills of households from the upper-income strata. Subsidization only takes place within each water company area, so that the firms are financially self-sufficient. Some public funds are available from central and departmental government budgets to help fund subsidies in areas where the majority of customers fall into the lower-income strata.

The errors of exclusion and inclusion for the Chilean and Colombian subsidies appear to be substantial, although the results depend on exactly who is defined as poor (bottom quintile or bottom two quintiles). Gomez-Lobo and Contreras (2000) show that the Colombian system (considering all three of the lower strata) is effective at reaching the poor, excluding only 5 percent of the poor. However, this comes at the cost of high errors of inclusion, with 80 percent of the beneficiaries being nonpoor households. The opposite pattern holds for the Chilean system, where errors of inclusion are comparatively low at 30 percent, but errors of exclusion are high at 80 percent.

Source: Gomez-Lobo and Contreras (2000).

Figure 4.3. *Break-Even Consumption for Infrastructure Service with Fixed Charges*

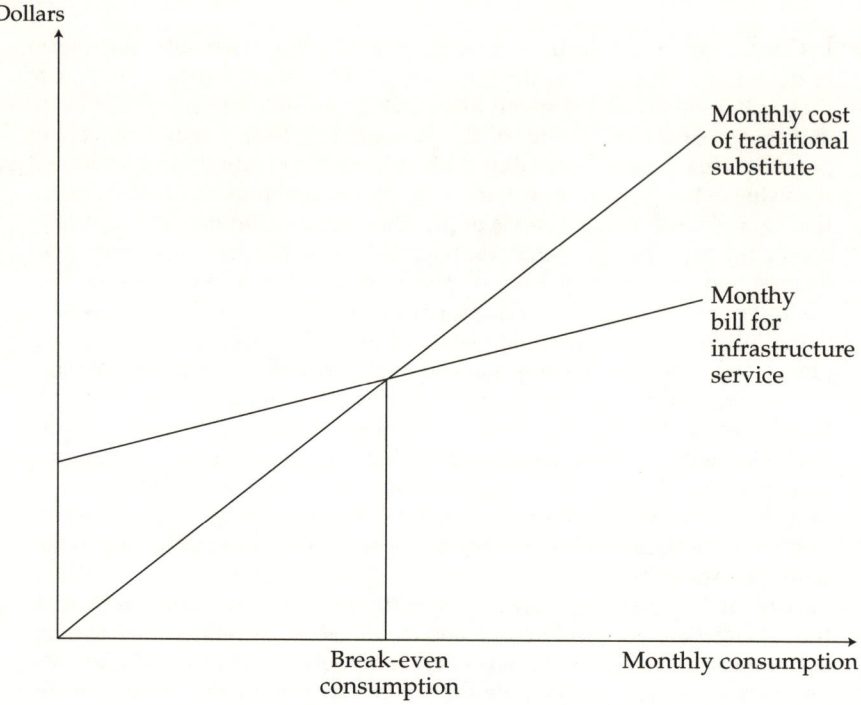

Source: Authors.

Reducing the Costs of Service

A second approach to improve affordability is to reduce the costs of the services rather than their charges. When technologically feasible, this approach has the advantage of not requiring any kind of subsidy. One possibility involves providing poor households with a lower quality of service. Another possibility entails placing physical limits on the volume of consumption by the poor.

Offering a service package with a lower cost and less service is sometimes desirable. In the telecommunications sector, the operator may provide low-income customers with telephones that can only receive incoming calls and make free (for example, 1-800) outgoing calls. In the electricity and water sectors, the quality of the connection can be reduced by promoting alternatives to conventional utilities (see chapter 3), or by providing lower delivery quality, for example, offering a cheaper service in exchange for accepting a higher probability of service interruptions. Anecdotal evidence suggests that in the case of rationing, operators are more likely to interrupt service to customers in low-income neighborhoods, who may be less vociferous in complaining about the inconvenience or may have less political power than better-off consumers. This double standard could be formalized, charging low-income households lower rates on the understanding that they would be more likely to encounter service interruptions. The state of Maryland in the United States offers this option, and finds many takers across income classes.

Technological devices may be used to keep utility bills within affordable limits. Because infrastructure services are always billed with a significant lag, households may find that monitoring and controlling their consumption over time is difficult. Consequently, their bills can be unpredictable, and can on occasion be unexpectedly large. For telephones, limiting the volume of the service that can be consumed in any given period is technologically feasible. For example, in Peru the private operator has introduced *lineas populares* (popular lines) with no connection charge, a flat usage fee, and a limited volume of monthly traffic (Melo 2000).

For water and electricity, service limiters limit the rate at which the service can be taken from the grid. EDF, France's electric utility, has implemented service limiters on a large scale since the mid-1990s (Wodon 2000c). This allows temporarily impoverished households to continue to consume a minimum of energy via a power limiter during a certain period, usually two months, the time technically required for energy aid funds to provide financial aid. The power limit was initially a 1-kilowatt ceiling on the amount of power that could be drawn at any one time, but has since been extended to 3 kilowatts. If the household does not accept the service limiter, it is disconnected. The system has reduced the number of disconnections by a third, from 600,000 to 400,000 residential customer disconnections per year from 1994 to 1995, and the number of disconnections has remained relatively stable since. While service limiters do not provide the same security as an overall limit on consumption, they may nonetheless help the poor reduce their consumption. However, service limiters have not yet been widely implemented in Latin America.

Facilitating Payment

In some cases the payment problem is due to a lack of financing rather than to affordability. In many countries infrastructure reforms occur during a structural reform of the economy, which results in significant increases in unemployment. Low-income households then face the problem of having little or no working capital to pay comparatively large and infrequent utility bills, and no savings or access to credit to continue paying bills when income temporarily declines as a result of illness or unemployment. Again, various alternatives can help households manage their resources over time and pay their bills. Two main approaches in developing countries deserve some attention: increasing the frequency of billing and introducing prepayment.

More Frequent Billing

The infrequency of billing for infrastructure services may create cash flow problems for poor households. A key difference between infrastructure services and non-network substitutes is the frequency with which consumers are required to pay. In the case of traditional alternatives, consumers typically pay small amounts to acquire one or two day's service at a time. With conventional utilities, billing is much less frequent, and the bill may be large in relation to the household's available cash. This can sometimes be resolved by shortening the payment cycle and increasing the frequency of billing. This increases the administrative costs of revenue collection for the operator, however, and raises the question of whether these additional costs should be recovered across the entire customer base or from poor customers only.

Prepayment meters are devices that disconnect service unless a charge is prepaid using either coins or a "smart card" (much the way that a public telephone works). Such devices have been used in countries of the Organisation for Economic Co-operation and Development, where they have been the subject of some criticism on the grounds that they are a way to conceal service disconnections. However, the technology allows prepayment meters to be equipped with built-in service limiters, so that disconnection need not be the alternative to nonpayment. Also the term prepayment meter may be misleading, as an initial level of consumption can be provided before payment, so that advance payment is not required. In Latin America prepaid cellular telephones have become extremely popular (Melo 2000). Prepayment meters for electricity and water services have so far mostly been used in the United Kingdom and South Africa, however. Unfortunately, this technology is much more expensive for electricity and water than for telephones, and hence may not always represent a cost-effective solution.

In Bolivia the number of mobile telephone subscribers increased 10-fold between 1996 and 1999, with an average annual rate of 66,000 new connections each year. The introduction of prepayment cards in 1998 appears to have been a great stimulus to demand, with prepaid telephones accounting for 86 percent of the increase in cellular use in 1998 and 1999. Anecdotal evidence suggests that prepayment cards have brought cellular phones within the reach of small entrepreneurs, who purchase the devices mainly for receiving business-related incoming calls.

Other Alternatives

Many other possibilities exist to facilitate payment by low-income customers, and Europeans have been quite creative in this context. The most useful services need not be the most costly. Box 4.3 lists the main energy assistance programs used by EDF, France's electric utility. Using annual surveys of a representative sample of its customers with payment difficulties, EDF found that a private appointment at the agency is the most appreciated service, whereas local neighborhood meetings to discuss energy-related issues appear to be the least useful. This type of information and the household surveys on which it is based are clearly useful for adapting energy assistance programs to the priorities of low-income customers. Household satisfaction surveys can also be used to assess the performance of a utility's local service centers, as these may differ markedly in the quality of services provided.

Targeting an Instrument

The evidence reviewed here suggests that many policy instruments widely used to improve the affordability of infrastructure services to poor households are actually badly targeted and often fail to benefit the poor. Techniques are needed to test the targeting properties of alternative social tariff policies and seek the most effective combination of eligibility criteria.

Eligibility Criteria

As mentioned in boxes 4.1 and 4.2, targeting performance is often analyzed using simple summary statistics, such as errors of inclusion and exclusion for a given targeting mechanism. A generalization of this approach uses relative operating characteristics (ROC) curves to assess which indicators (lifeline or various means-testing mechanisms) have the best performance.

Box 4.3. *Creativity in the Design of Low-Income Energy Assistance Programs*

France's electric utilities, Electricité de France (EDF) and Gaz de France (GDF), have a wide range of services for the poor. Not all programs have the same impact or importance, but the variety of initiatives implemented by EDF shows how creativity can help.

Service limiter: This technical device places a limit on the amount of electricity that can be consumed at any point. The service limiter is an alternative to disconnection, and it is available for a limited period, in principle while waiting for social worker assistance or for financial assistance.

Prepayment meter: The meter requires the user to pay at home using coins, prepaid cards, or a credit card. This meter allows consumption to be measured, and its cost to be evaluated more easily, thereby encouraging sound budget management. The disadvantage is that the client can be disconnected by not paying (but service limiter technology could be built in).

- *Person to contact for technical problems.* During a visit or a phone call, an EDF agent gives the name of a contact person at the local service center who can answer technical questions.
- *Invitation to a local meeting.* EDF organizes information meetings in poor neighborhoods to help poor customers learn how to better manage their energy consumption. The meetings also help improve the relationship between EDF and its customers, especially when EDF has had bad press, for example, because of disconnections.
- *Energy-saving advice.* EDF employees give advice, including information about the electricity consumption of consumers' appliances.
- *Insulation advice.* Advice is given on improving insulation and reducing heating costs.
- *800 telephone number.* Free phone calls to EDF can be made through a 1-800 number.
- *Payment deadline flexibility.* To adapt to irregular income flows among the poor, EDF accepts piecemeal "à la carte" payments; customers pay small amounts whenever they can.
- *Monthly payment.* EDF encourages automated monthly payment to avoid large six-month bills that poor customers cannot settle in a single payment.
- *Cash payment at local agency.* The poor pay part or all of their bill over the counter at their local EDF-GDF service center to maximize payment flexibility.
- *Right price advice.* An EDF employee informs customers about the various contracts (tariffs) available and advises on the contract best adapted to customers' needs and resources.

(box continues on following page)

Box 4.3. *(continued)*

- *Assistance in reading and understanding bills.* An EDF employee can explain the bill to customers who are illiterate or who have trouble understanding the bill.
- *Personalized contact at the service center.* Low-income customers are welcomed in a personalized way to discuss issues at the local service center, instead of being served by an anonymous employee behind a counter.
- *Appointments at a convenient time.* EDF centers remain open in the evening or on Saturday morning to facilitate making appointments for clients who are in default of payment.
- *Appointments held in private.* Space is reserved at the EDF center to meet with customers privately when discussing issues, just like in a bank.

Source: Wodon (2000b).

The idea is to use regressions to assess how the various targeting indicators predict the probability of being poor, and to ascertain how the two types of errors (exclusion of some poor households and inclusion of some nonpoor households) vary according to the choice of indicators used to determine eligibility. The methodology is described in box 4.4.

For each indicator that can be used for targeting, one associates a curve that plots the probability that a poor household will be classified as poor against the probability that a nonpoor household will be classified as poor for every possible value given to the indicator. Note that the indicator can be complex, and may actually consist of a combination of indicators, as the regression can be multivariate. If the ROC curve lies on the 45 degree line, the model has no predictive power, because the probability that a poor household be classified as poor is no higher than the probability that a nonpoor household be classified as poor. The more the ROC curve bows upward, the greater the model's predictive power. A summary measure of predictive power is the area under the ROC curve. If the area is larger than 50 percent, then the model has some predictive power; an area of 100 percent implies that the model predicts poverty perfectly.

The methodology was used to assess how well various indicators performed for identifying the poor among a sample of households with a

Box 4.4. *Targeting the Poor Using ROC Curves*

Denote by P, P^-, and P^+ the number of the poor, the number of the poor classified as nonpoor, and the number of the poor classified as poor by a model. Also denote by NP, NP^-, and NP^+, the number of the nonpoor, the number of the nonpoor classified as nonpoor, and the number of the nonpoor classified as poor. Sensitivity $SE = P^+/(P^- + P^+) = P^+/P$ is the fraction of poor households classified as poor. Specificity $SP = NP^-/(NP^- + NP^+) = NP^-/NP$ is the fraction of nonpoor households classified as nonpoor. The errors of inclusion and exclusion are thus $1 - SP$ and $1 - SE$.

	Nonpoor	*Poor*
Predicted nonpoor	$SP = NP^-/(NP^- + NP^+)$	$1 - SE = P^-/(P^- + P^+)$
Predicted poor	$1 - SP = NP^+/(NP^- + NP^+)$	$SE = P^+/(P^- + P^+)$

When using a statistical package and running a probit or logit regression for poverty, each observation is given an index value equal to the predicted right-hand side of the regression. This predicted value is used to classify the households as poor or nonpoor, with the computer typically using one-half as the cut-off point (those above the cut-off point are classified as poor). But this cut-off point can be changed. A ROC curve is a graph that plots SE as a function of $1 - SP$ for alternative values of the cut-off point. The figure below shows ROC curves. At the origin, $c = 1$, $SE = 0$, and $SP = 1$. At the upper right corner, $c = 0$, $SE = 1$, and $SP = 0$. The higher the ROC curve, the better its predictive power (a 45 degree line has no predictive power, while a vertical line from the origin to the top of the box followed by a horizontal line until the upper right corner has perfect predictive power). The area below a ROC curves provides a summary statistic of the predictive value of the underlying model. An area of 0.5 corresponds to the 45 degree line, which has no explanatory power. An area of 1.0 corresponds to perfect prediction.

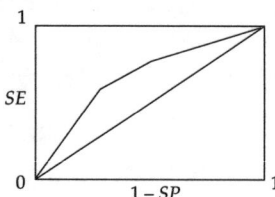

If the ROC curve of one targeting indicator (or set of indicators) lies above the ROC curves of all the alternatives, that indicator will typically be the best to target the poor for the class of social welfare functions based on the two types of errors that can be committed through targeting. If two ROC curves intersect, the choice of the best indicator will depend on the normative weights the policymaker attaches to the two types of errors.

Source: Wodon (1997).

connection to the electricity grid in Honduras (table 4.2) (Wodon, Ajwad, and Siaens 2000). The best results (the largest areas under the ROC curve) are obtained using a combination of different characteristics. Among single characteristics, electricity consumption has some predictive power, but less than other variables. In some cases, one can find an eligibility criterion that outperforms all others in terms of inclusion and exclusion errors. In other cases there are tradeoffs, and some weighting scheme is needed. In such cases the ROC curve can help select the best indicator for any given weighting scheme (see Wodon 1997; Wodon, Ajwad, and Siaens 2000).

Apart from the errors of inclusion and exclusion, the choice of targeting and funding mechanisms for subsidies depends on a number of other factors, including administrative costs, financing mechanisms, the political economy, and cost-effectiveness of subsidy systems.

Administrative Costs

One possibility for reducing the administrative costs of means-testing is to use a single screening system for many different welfare programs. In Chile an interview-based socioeconomic scoring system (known as the CAS index)

Table 4.2. *Areas under ROC Curves for Alternative Eligibility Criteria, Honduras*

(percent)

Criterion	Performance in identifying the extreme poor	Performance in identifying the poor
Socioeconomic status (multiple characteristics)	87	83
Demographics	72	71
Educational attainment	71	72
Employment status	69	66
Geographic location (department)	66	63
Housing characteristics (multiple characteristics)	82	81
Size of house	77	77
Quality of house	72	72
Access to electricity	68	69
Access to water and sanitation	61	58
Electricity consumption	70	73

Note: A larger percentage indicates better targeting performance.
Source: Wodon, Ajwad, and Siaens (2000).

is used to determine eligibility for subsidy. The cost of interviews is $8.65 per household. The Ministry of Planning estimates that 30 percent of Chilean households were interviewed, which seems reasonable given that the target group for the subsidy programs is the poorest 20 percent of the population. The CAS index is used as a targeting instrument not only for water subsidies, but also for the family income subsidy, the social housing subsidy, and the pension subsidy scheme. Because the fixed administrative costs are spread across several programs, the CAS is cost-effective. In 1996 administrative costs represented a mere 1.2 percent of the benefits distributed using the CAS score. If the water subsidy scheme had to bear all the administrative costs of the CAS system , these costs would represent 17.8 percent of the value of the subsidies (Gomez-Lobo and Contreras 2000).

In making decisions about the design of subsidy schemes, comparing alternative systems in terms of their cost-effectiveness in reaching the target population is useful. Gomez-Lobo and Contreras (2000) propose a simple formula to compare the cost-effectiveness of alternative subsidy mechanisms (see box 4.5). It relies on an effectiveness of resources invested index,

---

Box 4.5. *Comparing the Cost-Effectiveness of Subsidy Schemes*

Let *s* represent the subsidy received by each beneficiary household *i*. *I* is an index function that takes a value of one if the beneficiary household belongs to the government's target group and zero otherwise. The parameter θ is a household-specific weight that allows some households to be given greater consideration than others, according to their position in the income distribution. Finally, α captures the proportion of total expenditure that is absorbed by administrative costs, and λ represents the cost of raising public funds. The value of the effectiveness of resources invested index is bounded between zero and one. A value of zero implies that none of the subsidy funds reach the target group. A value of one implies (implausibly) that no leakage occurs beyond the target group and there are no administration and fund raising costs.

$$ERI = \frac{\sum_i \theta_i s_i I_i}{\left(\sum_i s_i\right)(1 + \alpha)(1 + \lambda)}$$

Source: Gomez-Lobo and Contreras (2000).

which is a ratio of benefits to costs. The benefits of the subsidy scheme are defined as the share of funds allocated to the target population that actually reach the target population. The costs of the scheme include the total value of the cash transfers made, the administrative costs, and the distortions imposed on the economy by raising the taxation revenues needed to finance the scheme. Using this index, Gomez-Lobo and Contreras (2000) show that the Colombian water subsidy is four to five times more efficient than the Chilean water subsidy. The Chilean scheme reaches a maximum score of 53 percent depending on how different members of the population are weighted.

Financing Mechanisms

Subsidies can be financed either directly from the public purse or by other customers through cross-subsidies. Cross-subsidies can themselves be administered in a variety of ways. One option used in Colombia is giving eligible households a percentage discount on their bills, which is funded by a percentage surcharge applied to ineligible households. Another approach is to apply a universal percentage levy on all bills. The money raised then goes into a special fund from which subsidies can be paid to households that apply and meet the eligibility criteria. Because they are somewhat hidden, cross-subsidies often have the advantage of generating less opposition from those who pay the subsidies than general taxes, and they avoid the problem of tax evasion. However, cross-subsidies may generate larger economic distortions than general taxes, because the prices both those receiving and paying the subsidies face are distorted. In any case, general taxes can also distort economic incentives (such as for labor supply and savings).

Political Economy

To avoid opposition from those who pay cross-subsidies, the subsidies should not be too large. In Colombia the principle of building equity considerations into utility tariffs was ratified by the 1991 Constitution. However, the 1994 Public Services Law, which laid the foundations for sector reform across the utilities, set limits for the magnitude of subsidies and surcharges to be applied to each socioeconomic group. These changes were motivated by a desire to harmonize practices across the country and the need to reduce the extent of cross-subsidies, which had grown to high levels that could become unsustainable in public opinion. Today the extent of subsidies and surcharges across different company areas vary greatly, and the level of the subsidies and surcharges remains higher than the maximum legally allowed.

While subsidies can help make infrastructure services available to the poor, they are a short-term solution while governments put into place systems that allow more efficient cash transfers for poverty reduction. According to economic theory, giving a household a cash transfer is generally preferable to using the same money to subsidize the price of a good. The reasoning is that a cash transfer leaves the household free to spend the money according to its own priorities, while the household can only benefit from the price reduction when it consumes the good in question.

To put the inefficiency of infrastructure subsidies into perspective, it is useful to quantify the welfare loss from subsidies versus cash transfers (see box 4.6). This requires making some assumptions on the form of the household's utility function, the expenditure share of the subsidized good, and the magnitude of the subsidy as a proportion of the price of the good. With a Cobb-Douglas utility function, for example, a subsidy of 80 percent applied to a good representing 10 percent of the household's consumption generates only 44 percent of the welfare gain that would have been achieved at the same cost with a cash transfer. The relative inefficiency of subsidies as opposed to cash transfers increases when the expenditure share of the subsidized good decreases, and increases when the unit price reduction provided by the subsidy increases. The efficiency losses associated with subsidies can be avoided, however.

One way to avoid the efficiency losses is to design the subsidies so that they apply to intramarginal consumption. This was done in the Illinois Residential Affordable Payment Program in the United States, a subsidy scheme begun in 1985. The objective was to limit program beneficiaries' cost of basic energy needs such as heating to no more than 8 percent of their income, and other energy needs to no more than 4 percent of their income. The program was accessible to households whose income was no higher than 125 percent of the poverty line. The program required households to pay the full price for energy if their consumption was above a level considered adequate for a household with their characteristics. The household's invoice was thus computed as $E = bY + PsQe$, where E is the invoice, b is the percentage of income to be devoted to energy, Y is the household income, Ps is the market price for electricity, and Qe is the excess consumption by the household above the level considered adequate given its characteristics (this level can be estimated using regression analysis). Costello (1988) shows how such a program avoids the problems associated with subsidies versus cash transfers.

Box 4.6. *Comparing the Welfare Gain from Cash Transfers
and Price Subsidies*

The advantage of income transfers over price subsidies can be illustrated
using the simplest optimization problem and utility function. Consider a
household with a Cobb-Douglas utility function $U = Q_1^\alpha Q_2^{1-\alpha}$ to be maxi-
mized under the budget constraint $P_1Q_1 + P_2Q_2 = B$. The first good is energy,
while the other good represents all other consumption sources. From the
first-order conditions, it can be shown that at the optimum $Q_1 = \alpha B/P_1$, while
the demand for the other goods is $Q_2 = (1 - \alpha)B/P_2$. This is the well-known
result for a Cobb-Douglas function: the expenditure shares are proportional
to the elasticities α and $1 - \alpha$. Consider now a subsidy a for energy such that
the budget constraint becomes $aP_1Q_1 + P_2Q_2 = B$, with $a < 1$. The demand for
energy becomes $Q_1 = \alpha B/(aP_1)$, while that for the other good remains at $Q_2 = (1 - \alpha)B/P_2$. The increase in utility obtained by the household thanks to the
price reduction for energy could also have been obtained with an income X
such that:

$$\left[\frac{(1-\alpha)B}{P_2}\right]^{1-\alpha}\left[\frac{\alpha B}{aP_1}\right]^{\alpha} = \left[\frac{(1-\alpha)X}{P_2}\right]^{1-\alpha}\left[\frac{\alpha X}{P_1}\right]^{\alpha}$$

It can be shown that $X = B/a^\alpha$. Without a subsidy, $a = 1$, $X = B$. With the
subsidy, $X - B = B(1 - a^\alpha)/a^\alpha$. Denote the transfer needed to reach X by $\Delta B = X - B$. The cost of the subsidy for the energy producer is $\alpha B(1 - a)/a$, which is
denoted by ΔC. The ratio of the cost of increasing utility through a transfer
versus a subsidy is $\Delta B/\Delta C = (1 - a^\alpha)a^{1-\alpha}/[(1 - a)\alpha]$. The gain in using a transfer as opposed to a subsidy is the largest when both the share of consump-
tion devoted to the good is small (parameter α) and the price reduction for
the good is large (one minus subsidy parameter a). Because the share of total
expenditures devoted to infrastructure services is often low, even mild subsidies can have large efficiency losses if no externalities such as health are
associated with subsidies.

Source: Wodon (2000a).

Concluding Comments

The political challenge of reform hinges on the importance of ensuring that
infrastructure services are at least as affordable after the reform as before.
While an increase in service quality and coverage may result in an increase
in the average tariff level, affordability for the poorest should remain at the
core of policy concerns. This is why the main regulatory challenge is often

to devise a scheme that ensures both affordability and reasonable guarantees of cost recovery for the operators. The empirical evidence indicates that many of the existing cross-subsidy schemes applied to electricity and water services are not particularly effective at reaching the poor, with a significant volume of resources leaking away to richer households.

Cost reductions combined with long and flexible commitments to private network operators or credible local alternative providers are the optimal solution. Creativity in tariff and subsidy design is clearly needed, and such creativity is apparent in Latin America. What may be missing is the marketing of reform. Costs can only be cut if technical and commercial losses (such as stealing and failures to pay bills) are reduced from their historical trends. This requires a better understanding of the amount that poor users are willing to pay. Once that is known, managing the willingness to pay though educational campaigns will require government support that enforces the payment obligation that is deemed reasonable and is included in the tariff design.

Increasingly, operators are allocating resources to promote the transparency of their management decisions. They are also increasingly investing in educating poor customers about what drives costs and ways of reducing them. Governments need to get more involved. Just as the ministries of finance in most countries create information campaigns to sell tax reforms, information campaigns about infrastructure reform could help ensure that the choices are well informed. Nongovernmental organizations, the media, and local associations have proven to be effective counterparts for operators when well informed. Such an education strategy is important, because affordability is partly an information problem. Because it is also an emotional concept, political support is needed to ensure that the policy choices aimed at helping the poor do so in a sustainable manner that benefits, and is fair to, all parties involved. This is the cornerstone of a realistic strategy aimed at minimizing the risks of excluding the poor from the benefits of infrastructure reform. The next chapter discusses analytical tools needed to establish priorities within this strategy.

5

Establishing Priorities

The previous chapters have shown the achievements of infrastructure reform, highlighted the challenges that lie ahead, and indicated possibilities for improvement. The challenges and opportunities are somewhat overwhelming for the Latin American region. While every politician and potential user will want immediate, affordable access for all, the extent of need is still so large, current public resources are still so limited, and the likelihood of having the private sector take on all the risks so remote, that priorities and a strategy to implement them are essential.

The main challenge in designing a strategy is that the objectives of access and affordability are not completely independent. Having access to a service that is not subsequently affordable serves no purpose. Furthermore, the lower the cost of the infrastructure service relative to the available substitutes, the more desirable promoting access becomes. This does not mean that the two objectives are necessarily in opposition. Both access and affordability can be simultaneously improved by choosing suitable policy instruments. Budget constraints do exist, however. If limited government subsidy funds must be allocated between connection and consumption subsidies, or if cross-subsidies are used to reduce access costs at the expense of raising service charges, tradeoffs arise.

The objectives of this chapter are threefold. It aims to help policymakers

- Diagnose the extent of access and consumption affordability and assess their relative importance and degree of urgency
- Set priorities within a sector and across sectors
- Choose the best instruments possible while explicitly recognizing the relevance of cost-effectiveness in the choice of instrument in a fiscally constrained environment.

The starting point for preparing a strategy or action plan is to establish whether poor households have a genuine problem in not being able to afford connection costs or paying for a subsistence level of consumption once connected. Several indicators can be used to determine this. These indicators are relatively straightforward to calculate using sector statistics and household survey data, and can help to identify the relative importance of access versus affordability.

Diagnostic Tools for Access

To be useful to policymakers and allow a strategic approach to addressing the needs of the poor in relation to utilities, an assessment of the level of access needs to answer three broad questions:

- What is the level of service coverage among poor households?
- Is the access problem for the poor primarily due to demand- or supply-side factors?
- Can the poor afford the initial costs associated with connecting to the network?

What Is the Level of Service Coverage among Poor Households?

If coverage among the poor is low, this may suggest that policies to promote access should be a higher priority than policies to promote affordability. This is because any policy targeted toward affordability will primarily benefit existing users of the service, and if most connected users are relatively well off, the policies will fail to benefit the neediest. The extent of the deficit in access to services depends on the service considered, the country, and whether the area is rural or urban. As mentioned in chapter 3, access rates are much higher and more equitable in urban than in rural areas; however, coverage in rural areas differs from country to country.

Figures 5.1 and 5.2 illustrate access patterns across income deciles for electricity and water services in seven Latin American countries. In Mexico, even in the poorest income decile (defined within rural sectors rather than nationally), three-fourths of the population had access to electricity, versus one-fifth of the population in the same decile in rural Guatemala. The Guatemalan households without access to electricity rely predominantly on kerosene or candles for lighting and batteries for powering small appliances such as radios, and this may be more efficient in remote areas if the cost of new connections is prohibitive. Such statistics are useful for

Figure 5.1. *Electricity Coverage Rates by Decile, Selected Countries, about 1998*

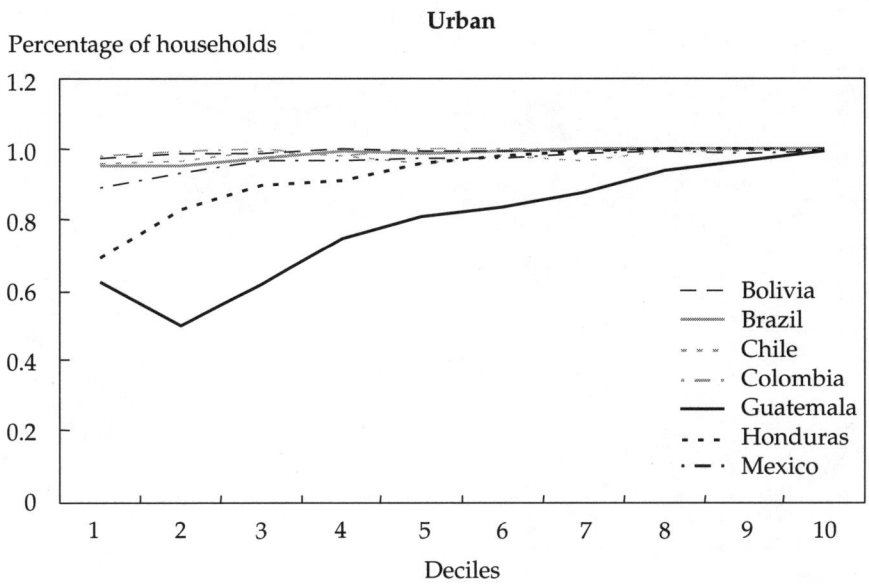

Urban

Percentage of households

Deciles

- – Bolivia
- Brazil
- Chile
- Colombia
- Guatemala
- Honduras
- Mexico

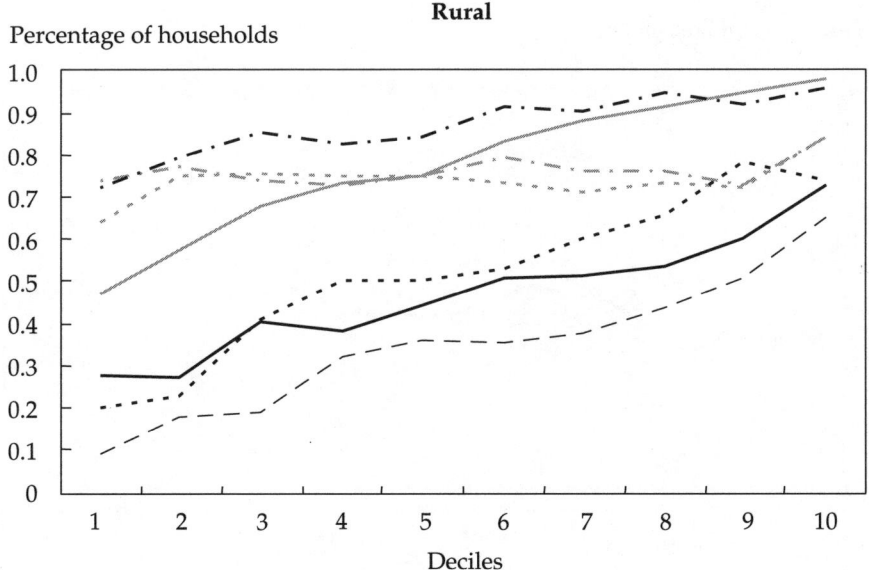

Rural

Percentage of households

Deciles

Source: National household surveys for each country.

Figure 5.2. *Water Coverage Rates by Decile, Selected Countries, about 1998*

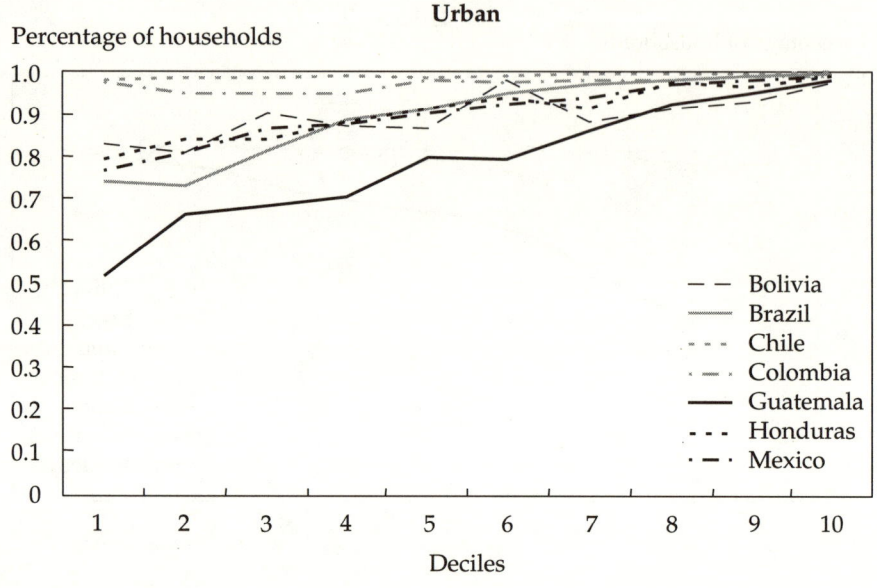

Urban

Percentage of households

Deciles

Legend:
- – – Bolivia
- Brazil
- · · · Chile
- · – · Colombia
- —— Guatemala
- · · · Honduras
- · – · Mexico

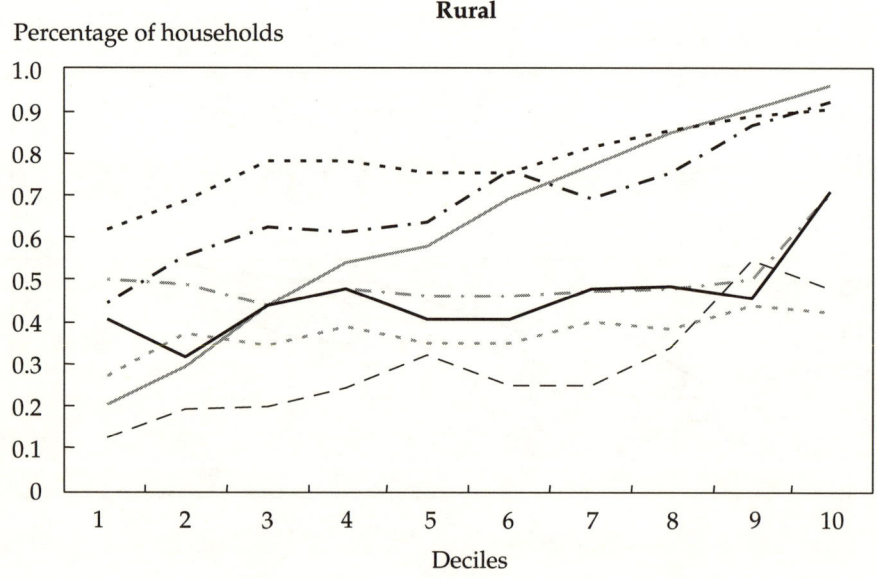

Rural

Percentage of households

Deciles

Source: National household surveys for each country.

estimating the absolute and relative size of the access problem, but they indicate little about the source of the problem, and hence about possible policy actions. For further details on the evolution of access patterns across income deciles over time see appendix 5.1.

Is the Lack of Access among the Poor due to Demand- or Supply-Side Factors?

A household may not be using a particular service either because the service is not available in the local community, or because the household chooses not to use the service even though it is available, for example, because it is not affordable or convenient. Being able to distinguish between these two situations is important for policy purposes, because the first suggests the need for supply-side interventions and the second the need for demand-side policy measures.

As indicated in table 5.1, about 60 percent of Guatemalan households in the first income decile live in communities with access to the electricity grid, but only 30 percent of these households actually use electricity. This implies that the take-up rate for electricity among households that have the option of using it is only 50 percent, indicating that the lack of access to electricity in Guatemala may be caused in part by demand-side problems.

In Honduras, the variable used to determine availability in the community is whether the streets have public lighting. Note that take-up may be overestimated, because some communities may have access, but no street lighting. A revised take-up rate was computed by dividing the assumed take-up at the decile level by the maximum take-up (for decile 6). In Guatemala, as in Honduras, the poor apparently have a lower take-up rate, which justifies action on the demand side.

Can the Poor Afford the Initial Costs of Connecting to the Network?

A poor household failing to connect to an infrastructure service once it is provided may reflect a rational choice, if the costs associated with connecting exceed the benefits. The costs of connecting to an infrastructure service can indeed be substantial, including connection charges and complementary investments the household must make in capital equipment and domestic installations, such as plumbing and wiring. The benefits of connecting can also be substantial, however, and could include reductions in the unit cost of services, including the costs of time spent gathering water or fuel, and improvements in quality and reliability. Nevertheless, even when a

Table 5.1. *Take-Up of Electricity, Guatemala and Honduras, 1999*

Income decile	Guatemala (national survey)			Honduras (survey of poor municipalities only)			
	Access (1)	Usage (2)	Take-up (3) = (2)/(1)	Access (1)	Usage (2)	Take-up (3) = (2)/(1)	Revised take-up
1	0.60	0.30	0.50	0.07	0.07	0.97	0.68
2	0.72	0.29	0.41	0.11	0.10	0.89	0.62
3	0.77	0.43	0.56	0.14	0.13	0.95	0.66
4	0.78	0.44	0.56	0.15	0.21	1.41	0.99
5	0.86	0.53	0.62	0.20	0.25	1.25	0.87
6	0.86	0.62	0.72	0.23	0.32	1.43	1.00
7	0.89	0.67	0.75	0.31	0.41	1.31	0.92
8	0.93	0.76	0.82	0.42	0.56	1.36	0.95
9	0.95	0.86	0.90	0.47	0.62	1.31	0.92
10	0.98	0.95	0.97	0.54	0.69	1.29	0.90
Overall	0.86	0.64	0.74	0.26	0.34	1.28	0.90

Note: In Honduras, the revised take-up is the take-up divided by the maximum take-up.
Source: Authors' estimates.

network connection is economically attractive, poor households—which typically have no savings and lack access to credit—may be unable to finance the initial investments.

As discussed earlier in the context of privatizing water supply in Argentina, some evidence suggests that access costs may be more of a barrier than use of service costs. When this is the case, social policies to subsidize tariffs to users of the service may be the wrong choice. The relative importance of access costs can be assessed in several ways, as the following examples illustrate.

To assess the extent to which electricity connections may be unaffordable to poor households, expressing the start-up costs for each alternative fuel as a proportion of the monthly income of the poorest is useful. While traditional fuels such as candles and kerosene have almost no start-up costs, the connection charge for electricity in Guatemala is $146, which represents about one month's income for a household of five people on the extreme poverty line. This suggests that to expand electricity access in Guatemala, policymakers need to find ways to reduce start-up costs.

Access to telephones among poor Peruvian households has increased dramatically despite an increase in user charges. This is partly because of a reduction in the initial costs of a connection. Following the privatization of Telefonica in 1993, residential connection charges fell from $493 in 1994 to $251 in 1998. Simultaneously, the cost of basic monthly services almost tripled, from $5.86 to $14.90, because of a rebalancing between local and long-distance charges (Melo 2000). The percentage of low-income households with a telephone increased from 1 percent to 21 percent during this period. While other factors such as economic growth must surely have contributed to this growth, these figures suggest that increasing monthly charges may be less a barrier to the poor than connection charges.

These examples show how relatively simple tests can help avoid discrimination against the poor. Such tests relating monthly cost to monthly income should be standard. They should be simple to put together from information relatively easily available from any operators and the income surveys produced by statistical offices in most countries in the region. Simple and cheap sampling techniques can also be good substitutes for official surveys.

Diagnostic Tools for Affordability

An assessment of the state of affordability must answer the following three questions:

- How much are the poor *able* to pay for utility services?
- How much are the poor *willing* to pay for utility services?
- Are utility payment cycles for the poor synchronized with their income cycles?

How Much Are the Poor Able to Pay?

As obvious as it seems, reformers often forget a basic test of ability to pay. Designing a tariff or providing service at a level or quality that users cannot afford makes no sense, but few reformers demand studies that assess ability to pay. In most cases, the government has at least some information on the income level of potential users in every region affected by the reform. In the rare cases where it has no information, simple surveys can be conducted to provide a rough indication of income levels, which can then be compared with the expected average utility bill. Caution must be taken to consider all the services households need when assessing affordability, as reforms that influence all utilities simultaneously are not uncommon. The affordability test comparing total income to total bills must focus on the total potential bill under various tariff design scenarios, including various levels and types of subsidies the government might be considering.

How Much Are the Poor Willing to Pay?

A common erroneous assumption is that the poor are not willing to pay for services. As discussed earlier, the evidence suggests that the poor are willing to pay, and thus the commercial risk resulting from nonpayment is more limited than often argued. A revealing and sound indicator of willingness to pay is the amount that the poor actually pay for alternatives to network providers. This gives a benchmark against which the tariff a utility plans to charge can be compared, and can be helpful in designing the specific tariff or targeting subsidies. This information can also help policymakers take decisions that would be politically risky without the proper supporting research.

In practice, policymakers should be able to rely on three main sources of information about willingness to pay:

- Willingness to pay surveys
- Implicit expenditure savings
- Hedonic rental regressions.

WILLINGNESS TO PAY SURVEYS. Surveys can be used to estimate households' willingness to pay to obtain the service. This willingness to pay can then be compared with the actual cost of the service. This approach was applied for the water sector to households in the first three deciles of Panama's income distribution (households considered poor). The results illustrated in figure 5.3 indicate that the average willingness to pay among poor households was $0.46 per cubic meter, well above the existing tariff level of $0.21 per cubic meter (Foster, Gomez-Lobo, and Halpern 2000), suggesting no major affordability problem at the existing tariff.

This type of information has been standard in most water, sanitation, and transport projects financed by the multilaterals in the region. Project files contain treasure troves of demand studies, often including disaggregation by income group. Such willingness to pay studies have been conducted in Brazil since the mid-1980s, and have been used to get projects approved. These studies did not, however, receive much attention from policymakers, even though they could probably have benefited politically

Figure 5.3. *Willingness to Pay for Water and Sanitation Services among Poor Households in Panama*

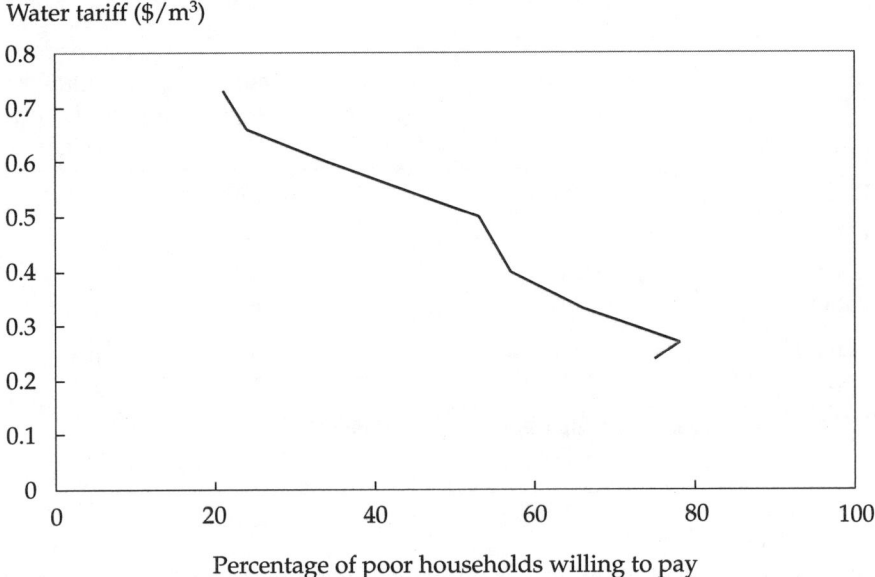

Water tariff ($/m³)

Percentage of poor households willing to pay

Source: Foster, Gomez-Lobo, and Halpern (2000).

from disseminating them via the media. A major step forward in documenting the demand side of the affordability problem would be to increase the transparency and dissemination of the information available.

EXPENDITURE DATA FROM HOUSEHOLD SURVEYS. One drawback with willingness to pay surveys is that they are based on hypothetical questions rather than on actual payment behavior. Consequently, existing expenditure patterns among households not connected to utility services should also be examined. As noted earlier, such households often pay much higher prices for traditional substitutes to utility services.

In Guatemala, subsistence consumption of electricity was defined as an allowance equivalent to one 60-watt light bulb and one 16-watt radio running for four hours each day. This allowance was based on consultation with local experts and was supported by empirical analysis of the energy consumption patterns of the poorest households. Subsistence electricity costs were found to be less than $1 per month, equivalent to less than 1 percent

Table 5.2. *Affordability of Electricity Consumption Using Data from Guatemala*

	Monthly cost of subsistence consumption		Cost of typical bill for subsistence consumption	
Energy source	Absolute cost (US$)	Relative cost (percentage of subsistence income)	Absolute cost (US$)	Relative cost (percentage of subsistence income)
Electricity	0.73	0.40	2.64	2.00
Substitutes				
Candles	93.60	62.40	n.a.	n.a.
Batteries	0.95	0.60	n.a.	n.a.
Total	94.55	63.00	n.a.	n.a.

n.a. Not applicable.
Source: Foster and Tre (2000); Foster, Tre, and Wodon (2000a).

of household income (table 5.2). However, meeting the same needs with candles and batteries would cost about 100 times as much and absorb nearly two-thirds of the household budget. Thus households without access to electricity are unable to meet energy subsistence requirements using traditional substitutes for electricity.

Such information can also be used to estimate the expenditure savings resulting from a utility connection (box 5.1 and table 5.3). The methodology is described in box 5.1, and results for Guatemala and Honduras are presented in table 5.3. In Honduras, a connection to the public electricity network resulted in a 19 percent decrease in energy expenditures, while in Guatemala, the effective price of energy was reduced by 25 to 31 percent when the household had access to electricity, although overall energy expenditure rose as a result of higher levels of energy use. These results can be used to estimate the value of the connection for the poor.

HEDONIC RENTAL REGRESSIONS. The value of a connection is measured from the difference in rental values between otherwise similar dwellings with or without connections. Box 5.2 describes the methodology and table 5.4 presents results for Bolivia, Guatemala, and Honduras. Each of the utility services added 15 to 60 percent to the rental value of the dwelling, with the premium for sanitation somewhat higher than for water and electricity. These rental premiums are equivalent to an appreciable percentage of the

Box 5.1. *Estimating the Value of a Connection Using Expenditure Data*

One methodology to assess the value of access quantifies the benefits of a connection in terms of whether it permits households to save on the expenditures required to meet their needs. Wodon and Ajwad (2000b) proposed this method using data for Honduras. The authors estimated a regression relating energy expenditures to household characteristics, including access to the electricity grid. Let T represent total energy expenditures, L a vector of geographic location dummies, H a vector of characteristics of the residents in the household, R a vector describing the physical characteristics of the residence, E a dummy variable for access to the electricity grid, and O a vector of dummies for access to other sources of energy. With a distribution of energy expenditures lognormal, the authors estimate the following regression:

$$\log(T_i) = \beta_0 + \beta_1 L_i + \beta_2 H_i + \beta_3 R_i + \beta_4 E_i + \beta_5 O_i + \varepsilon_i.$$

The coefficient β_4 captures the percentage change in energy expenditures for those with access to electricity. For Honduras, the estimated value for β_4 was equal to -0.46, representing a reduction in expenditures of 46 percent.

In some cases looking at the change in energy expenditures for households with and without connections may not be enough, because expenditures may increase if the price of energy is reduced with a connection and the price elasticity of demand is large. Also, from an econometric point of view, a connection to the grid may be correlated with unobserved variables that are themselves positively correlated with energy expenditures, so that a connection may be associated in the regression with higher instead of lower expenditures. To avoid these difficulties, it is possible to transform all sources of energy into common units of effective kilowatt hours, and to estimate three regressions for, respectively, total energy expenditures, total energy consumption (in efficient kilowatt hours), and price per effective kilowatt hour. Even though consumption may be higher with a connection, at least the price per effective kilowatt hour of energy consumed should decrease. Denoting by E_i the total energy consumption and by P_i the price per efficient kilowatt hour, the three regressions to be estimated are as follows:

$$\log(T_i) = \beta_0 + \beta_1 L_i + \beta_2 H_i + \beta_3 R_i + \beta_4 E_i + \beta_5 O_i + \varepsilon_i$$
$$\log(E_i) = \lambda_0 + \lambda_1 L_i + \lambda_2 H_i + \lambda_3 R_i + \lambda_4 E_i + \lambda_5 O_i + \upsilon_i$$
$$\log(P_i) = \gamma_0 + \gamma_1 L_i + \gamma_2 H_i + \gamma_3 R_i + \gamma_4 E_i + \gamma_5 O_i + \kappa_i.$$

Given that for all households $T_i = E_i P_i$, for all parameter estimates, $\beta_j = \lambda_j + \gamma_j$. If energy expenditures or prices are reduced with a connection to the grid, γ_4 will be negative and statistically different from zero. As shown in table 5.3, in Honduras a connection to the public electricity network was associated with a 19 percent decrease in expenditures. In Guatemala overall expenditures rose (which can be the result of price and income effects), but the price per effective kilowatt hour of energy fell by 25 to 31 percent.

Source: Wodon and Ajwad (2000b).

Table 5.3. Energy Expenditure Savings from a Connection,
Guatemala and Honduras, 1999

Percentage change in	Honduras, poor municipalities	Guatemala, urban	Guatemala, rural
Energy expenditure (1)	–0.19	+32.8	+61.4
Net energy consumption (2)	—	+56.3	+95.3
Effective price (1) – (2)	—	–24.9	–31.1

— Not available.
Source: Foster, Tre, and Wodon (2000a); Wodon, Ajwad, and Siaens (2000).

income of households at the bottom of the distribution of income. For example, providing all three services (electricity, water, and sanitation) to a first quintile household that previously had none of them would be equivalent to raising household income by 10 to 20 percent. If all households without access were to obtain access, and if the access were valued according to the rental value estimates, the share of the population in poverty would be reduced by 3 to 5 percent.

Are Utility Payment Cycles for the Poor Synchronized with Their Income Cycles?

Finally, in assessing the affordability of consuming infrastructure services, not only must the cost of meeting subsistence requirements be considered, but also the payment cycles and timing for each service. As discussed in chapter 4, unlike many of the traditional substitutes, infrastructure services are often purchased infrequently, requiring comparatively large payments, for example, a monthly electricity bill incorporating standing charges. Because poor households usually do not have financial reserves, these payments may be difficult to meet even when the daily cost of using the service is low compared with traditional alternatives. Consequently, the cost of meeting a typical infrastructure bill as a percentage of the monthly income of the poorest, based on local payment arrangements, is a relevant indicator.

Setting Access and Affordability Priorities

While the various analyses suggested earlier may reveal that policymakers are facing both affordability and access problems, as is quite common, only

---

Box 5.2. *Estimating the Value of a Connection Using Hedonic Rental Regressions*

To estimate the gain in rental value from access to electricity, water, and sanitary installations, Siaens and Wodon (2000) estimated the following regression with data from Bolivia, Guatemala, and Honduras:

$$\ln (R_i) = \beta_0 + \beta_1 L_i + \beta_2 U_i + \beta_3 H_i + \beta_4 E_i + \varepsilon_i$$

where R_i is the rent paid, L_i is the geographic location (vector of geographic dummies), U_i is a dummy variable that assumes a value of one when the household is in an urban area and a value of zero when it is in a rural area, H_i is a vector of dwelling characteristics, and E_i has information on access to electricity. The vector of dwelling characteristics includes the type of housing (house, apartment, shack, room, and so on); the type of material with which the walls and ground are built (stone or cement, wooden, earth, and so on); the type of access to water (public service, well, river, and so on); the type of access to sanitary equipment (latrine, sewerage, and so on); and the number of rooms.

Two important caveats may reduce the actual value of a connection. First, for those households that are tenants and pay rent, the method may not work, because the value of a connection is a benefit for the owner rather than the tenant. In a competitive rental market, an owner may increase the rent after receiving a connection, in which case the tenant does not gain. In practice, however, especially in poor rural areas, many of the poor are owners, even if the house is extremely modest. Second, for owners, while the value of a connection is received at the time of connection, the benefit is continuous. In other words, one could compute the one-shot value of the connection as the discounted stream over time of its benefits, and this one-shot value could be realized if the owner were to sell the house and move. At the same time, if the price of electricity includes a fixed charge, this fixed charge may have been computed to offset the cost of the connection for the utility over time. In this case, the connection offers no additional benefit, apart from the lack of rationing for the household for that good. Thus if the fixed term of the tariff structure is taken into account, the value of the connection is likely to be lower than what was estimated.

Source: Siaens and Wodon (2000).

---

limited fiscal resources are available to finance subsidies. The main question then becomes how to choose between access and consumption subsidies. Once more, simple rules can be used to choose between these two policy instruments (see box 5.3).

Table 5.4. *Poverty Reduction Impact of Household Connections to Infrastructure Services, Bolivia, Guatemala, and Honduras*

Category	Electricity			Water			Sanitation		
	Bolivia	Guatemala	Honduras	Bolivia	Guatemala	Honduras	Bolivia	Guatemala	Honduras
Percentage increase in rent	28.43	37.62	32.17	30.66	14.71	42.32	45.46	60.11	35.96
Percentage increase in income									
Quintile 1	2.47	2.62	7.22	3.44	1.00	7.32	11.07	3.86	11.01
Quintile 2	1.52	1.78	1.98	2.21	0.79	2.55	4.49	2.99	3.64
Quintile 3	1.50	1.47	1.33	1.89	0.66	1.67	3.94	2.59	2.56
Quintile 4	1.24	1.42	1.05	2.20	0.67	1.68	3.90	2.19	2.20
Quintile 5	1.23	1.19	0.64	1.87	0.63	1.27	4.63	2.21	1.57
Percentage change in extreme poverty									
National sample	−0.53	−4.91	−0.86	−1.18	−1.69	−0.32	−2.80	−8.86	−2.20
Households without access	−1.02	−0.58	−1.31	−2.19	−0.17	−1.51	−3.54	−2.17	−3.09
Percentage change in poverty									
National sample	−0.21	−7.31	−0.10	−0.42	−2.70	−0.17	−1.38	−8.98	−0.62
Households without access	−0.53	−0.98	−0.18	−0.98	−0.29	−0.92	−1.90	−2.27	−0.93

Source: Siaens and Wodon (2000).

Box 5.3. *Choosing between Consumption and Connection Subsidies*

To establish priorities between subsidizing new connections and providing consumption subsidies for those who already have access to an infrastructure service, a number of parameters must be taken into account. The optimal allocation rule depends on the social welfare function of the policymaker and a number of other parameters. In the simplest case, however—where (among other assumptions) the consumption subsidies are inframarginal, all poor households are weighted in the same way, no weight is placed on the welfare of the nonpoor, and there are no administrative costs—the decision to promote consumption versus connection subsides boils down to a comparison of four parameters.

Specifically, denoting by α_s and α_c the share of the consumption and connection subsidies that are obtained by the poor, by λ_s and λ_c the administrative costs as a share of total costs involved in targeting consumption and connection subsidies, by V the value of a connection for the poor, and by C the cost paid by the poor for their connection (which is equal to the full cost of the connection less the connection subsidy), connection or consumption subsidies should be promoted according to the following rule:

If $\dfrac{\alpha_S}{\alpha_C}\dfrac{(1-\lambda_S)}{(1-\lambda_C)} \leq \dfrac{V}{C}$, promote connection subsidies.

If $\dfrac{\alpha_S}{\alpha_C}\dfrac{(1-\lambda_S)}{(1-\lambda_C)} > \dfrac{V}{C}$, promote consumption subsidies.

If α_c is equal to α_s, and if λ_s is equal to λ_c, it is better to promote connections if the value for the poor of a connection (V) is larger than the cost they have to pay for the connection (C). The actual cost of a connection $C/(1-\lambda_c)$ increases with access rates, because at high access rates, those with no access tend to live in more remote areas. Hence, with higher access rates, at some point the balance is likely to favor consumption subsidies instead of connection subsidies.

Source: Wodon (2001).

Whether a government should promote connection or consumption subsidies depends on the following three main criteria:

- The relative targeting performance of both types of subsidies
- The administrative costs of both types of subsidies
- The value of a connection compared with its cost.

Relative Targeting Performance

As discussed in chapter 4, targeting tools are not perfect. Some leakage of subsidies to unintended beneficiaries will always occur, whether the subsidies are for connections or consumption. However, because connections tend to be concentrated among wealthier households, leakage is more likely to occur with consumption subsidies than with connection subsidies. However, connection subsidies are more likely to benefit the poor in urban than in rural areas, where even some of the better-off do not have connections.

Administrative Costs

The targeting performance of a subsidy depends on the indicator used for the subsidy, and a balance must be achieved between the cost of finding information for a better indicator and the gains in targeting achieved with a better indicator. For example, lifeline subsidies are much cheaper to implement than means-tested subsidies, but tend to be less effective at reaching the poor. Because a connection subsidy is a one-time transfer, the eligibility of the beneficiary household over time does not need to be re-evaluated. The total value of a connection subsidy also tends to be higher than the recurring value of a consumption subsidy. These two factors can make the administrative costs for connection subsidies lower than for consumption subsidies. Foster, Gomez-Lobo, and Halpern (2000) suggest that in Panama, administrative costs are worth 7 percent of total expenditures for connection subsidies versus 25 percent for consumption subsidies. In Chile, the stand-alone administrative costs of the water consumption subsidy would absorb 18 percent of program costs (Gomez-Lobo and Contreras 2000). However, the Chilean water subsidy scheme shares its screening procedure with numerous other social programs, so that the overall burden of administrative costs is as low as 1 percent.

Value of Connection Versus Cost

The third parameter to be considered is the ratio of the value of access for the poor to the cost of access net of the subsidy. When the value of a connection is larger for the poor than its cost to them, the government can provide more than $1 in value to the poor with $1 in spending on a connection policy. With subsidies, however, $1 in cost is worth at most $1 in subsidy. The hedonic rental value and the expenditure savings approaches discussed earlier can both help here.

However, both these methods may give underestimates of the value of a connection to a household if they do not take into account the dynamic benefits that a connection may bring to a household over time by improving its potential to generate income. A utility connection, for example, may improve the household's ability to generate income by enabling a more productive use of women's time or enhancing the scope for home-based businesses. Women liberated from the time-consuming task of gathering water or fuelwood can use their time more productively. Infrastructure services may also increase productivity in household-based microenterprises by allowing households to use power-assisted tools, lengthen the working day with illumination, and connect with business partners and customers by telephone.

Using panel data for Peru, Chong and Hentschel (1999) examined the influence of household utility connections on the growth of per capita consumption between 1994 and 1997, controlling for other factors. They found that households with utility connections experienced significantly faster growth than those without connections. Moreover, returns appeared to increase according to the number of services the household had. Households with two services experienced 10 percent higher consumption growth than those with none. Households with all utility services—electricity, water, sewerage, and telephone—experienced 37 percent higher growth. Electricity service had the single greatest impact on household welfare in rural areas, while telephone service had the greatest impact in urban areas.

Setting Infrastructure Sector Priorities

In most sectors government subsidies are likely to be part of the strategy designed to meet at least some of the total consumption needs of the poor in infrastructure, and establishing priorities between sectors is important. This can be done by looking at the impact of subsidies on poverty through consumption dominance (CD) curves. CD curves can be used to test the extent to which subsidizing different sectors helps reduce poverty (see box 5.4). As for the impact of subsidies on income distribution, this can be addressed by the decomposition of inequality indexes (for example, Gini indexes) by consumption sources.

The CD curve approach provides useful guidelines, and its principle is simple: if governments have a choice, they should subsidize goods consumed in larger proportion by the poor. Subsidies for water and urban transport, for instance, tend to have a greater poverty reduction potential than subsidies for electricity and telephone services, because the poor's share of

Box 5.4. *Assessing the Impact of Utility Subsidies on Poverty*

CD curves help analyze the impact of subsidies on poverty. As explained in Makdissi and Wodon (2000), the analysis is based on curves that plot the cumulative consumption share of a good for all households below a given level of income. If the CD curve for a specific service lies above that of a second infrastructure service everywhere, this means that poorer households consume a relatively large proportion of the first service compared with the second. This in turn implies that providing consumption subsidies for the first good and financing these subsidies from a tax on the second good reduces poverty. More generally, the higher the CD curve of a good, the more poverty reducing a subsidy will be. To assess which infrastructure subsidies should be favored for subsidies, it is thus sufficient to trace the CD curves of the various candidates.

The figure below compares urban and interprovincial public transportation in Bolivia. The CD curve for urban transportation lies above that for interprovincial transportation, indicating that the poor represent a larger share of the total expenditures devoted to urban as opposed to interprovincial public transportation. Therefore, for poverty reduction, subsidizing urban transportation is better than subsidizing interprovincial transportation, which is not surprising, because the poor rarely have the resources to travel to other provinces, while they do use public transportation within their own urban areas.

Public Transport: Urban Versus Interprovincial, 1999

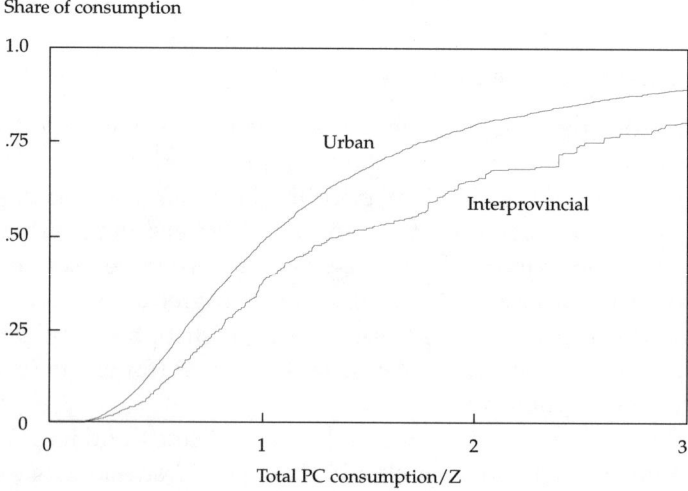

Source: Makdissi and Wodon (forthcoming).

Table 5.5. *Ranking Subsidies in Terms of Their Impact on Poverty (CD Curves)*

Country	1st (most poverty reducing)	2nd	3rd	4th (least poverty reducing)
Bolivia	Urban transport	Electricity and water	Interurban transport	Communications (telephones and postage)
Honduras	Water	Buses	Public telephones and electricity	Private telephones
Mexico	Public transport	Water	Electricity	Communications

Source: Makdissi and Wodon (forthcoming);Wodon (2000a).

total expenditures for water and urban transportation is larger than for electricity and telephone service. Table 5.5 presents results from applying the CD curve methodology using data from Bolivia, Honduras, and Mexico.

The impact on inequality of small changes in prices, subsidies, or taxes on commodities can be analyzed using the tools presented in box 5.5. An increase in the price or tax of a source of consumption whose Gini elasticity is larger (smaller) than one will decrease (increase) the inequality in per capita consumption. In Bolivia, for example, water, electricity, and public transport all have Gini coefficients of less than one, indicating that subsidizing these services can reduce inequality. In Honduras, where access rates for electricity are low, the existing electricity subsidies increase inequality.

The impact of subsidies on inequality and poverty may vary from one country to another (see table 5.6 for consumption sources and their Gini elasticities in Mexico). Table 5.6 suggests that to reduce inequality in Mexico, providing subsidies for water is preferable to providing subsidies for other items. Subsidies for electricity would be inequality neutral, while subsidies for telecommunications would increase inequality.

The Decision Tree

The various elements of a strategy discussed so far can be brought together into a decision tree that can be applied in the context of most typical reform

Box 5.5. *Assessing the Impact of Utility Subsidies on Inequality*

To analyze the impact of subsidies on inequality in per capita consumption, one can use a source decomposition of the Gini index proposed by Lerman and Yitzhaki (1985) (see also Garner 1993). Denote total per capita consumption by y, the cumulative distribution function for total per capita consumption by $F(y)$, and the mean total per capita consumption across all households by μ_y. The Gini index can be decomposed as follows:

$$G_y = 2\,cov\,[y,\,F(y)]/\mu_y = \Sigma_i\,S_iR_iG_i$$

where G_y is the Gini index for total consumption, G_i is the Gini index for consumption y_i from source i, $S_i = \mu_i/\mu_y$ is the share of total consumption obtained from source i, and R_i is the Gini correlation between consumption from source i and total consumption. The Gini correlation is defined as $R_i = cov\,[y_i,\,F(y)]/cov[(y_i,\,F(y_i)]$, where $F(y_i)$ is the cumulative distribution function of per capita consumption from source i. The Gini correlation R_i can take values between –1 and 1. Consumption from sources such as consumption from capital that tend to be strongly and positively correlated with total consumption will have large positive Gini correlations. Consumption from sources such as transfers tend to have smaller, and possibly negative, Gini correlations. The overall (absolute) contribution of a source of consumption i to the inequality in total per capita consumption is thus $S_iR_iG_i$.

The foregoing source decomposition provides a simple way to assess the impact on inequality in total consumption of a marginal percentage change equal for all households in consumption from a particular source or the price of that source. As proven by Stark, Taylor, and Yitzhaki (1986), the impact of increasing for all households the consumption (or price) from source i in such a way that y_i is multiplied by $(1 + e_i)$ where e_i tends to zero, is

$$\frac{\partial G_y}{\partial e_i} = S_i(R_iG_i - G_y).$$

This equation can be rewritten to show that the percentage change in inequality caused by a marginal percentage change in the consumption (or price) from source i is equal to that source's contribution to the Gini minus its contribution to total consumption. In other words, at the marginal level, what matters in evaluating the redistributive impact of consumption sources (or their prices) is not their Gini, but the product R_iG_i, which is called the pseudo Gini. Alternatively, denoting by $\eta_i = R_iG_i/G_y$ the so-called Gini elasticity of consumption for source i, the marginal impact of a percentage change in consumption (or price) from source i identical for all households on the Gini for total consumption in percentage terms can be expressed as

(box continues on following page)

Box 5.5. *(continued)*

$$\frac{\partial G_y / \partial e_i}{G_y} = \frac{S_i R_i G_i}{G_y} - S_i = S_i(\eta_i - 1) \cdot$$

Thus a percentage increase in the consumption (or price) from a source with a Gini elasticity η_i smaller (larger) than one will decrease (increase) the inequality in per capita consumption. The lower the Gini elasticity, the larger the redistributive impact of a utility subsidy.

Source: Wodon and Yitzhaki (forthcoming).

---

projects (figure 5.4). This tree is designed to help prioritize between access and affordability. It recognizes explicitly that prioritization depends primarily on the needs of the poor, but must also reflect the cost-effectiveness of the corresponding policies, in particular, when the scope of the poverty issues is overwhelming for a fiscally constrained government.

The first stage involves identifying whether access and affordability are serious problems using the indicators described earlier. If access is a problem, the instruments discussed in chapter 3 provide some solutions. If affordability is the problem, the instruments discussed in chapter 4 will help. The real challenge is that no matter which combination of instruments is selected, the need for government funding is likely to be significant. This introduces a budget constraint on the choice of instruments that is too often an afterthought. Therefore examining the relative cost-effectiveness of both types of policies is particularly important, both in terms of targeting the sector and administrative costs.

For consumption affordability, the CD curve and the Gini elasticities of utility consumption provide rough guidelines to help policymakers decide which sector to help first from the point of view of poverty and income distribution. Connection-oriented subsidies will tend to be more cost-effective to administer, and in many instances they are likely to be the preferred mode of intervention. This is not settled, however, and any reformer must investigate when deciding what to subsidize.

Table 5.6. *Source Decomposition of Consumption Gini in Mexico:*
Gini Elasticities, 1996

Source	Nation	Urban	Rural
Inequality increasing sources			
Other expenses	1.578	1.558	1.766
Culture and leisure	1.549	1.456	1.699
Private transport	1.526	1.474	1.806
Post, telegraph, phone	1.384	1.246	1.605
Furniture, tools	1.357	1.306	1.738
Imputed rent and charges	1.125	0.998	1.019
Education	1.181	1.082	0.868
Inequality neutral sources			
Other food and drinks	1.072	1.004	1.090
Tobacco and alcohol	1.053	1.090	1.003
Pasteurized milk	1.044	0.851	1.293
Auto consumption	1.039	1.005	0.934
Clothes and shoes	1.008	0.986	1.006
Domestic material	0.991	1.029	1.175
Electricity	0.952	0.842	1.043
Inequality decreasing sources			
Water	0.918	0.791	0.987
Cleaning	0.913	0.867	0.854
Meat and fish	0.750	0.605	0.977
Health expenditures	0.650	1.144	1.324
Public transport	0.612	0.432	0.983
Cheese, oils, etc.	0.488	0.419	0.604
Vegetables and fruits	0.478	0.431	0.545
Cereals	0.463	0.435	0.580
Other kinds of milk	0.398	0.252	0.944
Sugar, salt, etc.	0.340	0.383	0.459
Tortilla	0.120	−0.126	0.732
Subsidized milk	−0.343	−0.783	0.417
Free tortilla	−0.666	−1.042	0.341
Corn flour	−0.841	−0.262	−0.154

Source: Wodon and others (2000).

Figure 5.4. *Decision Tree for Prioritizing between Subsidizing Access or Consumption*

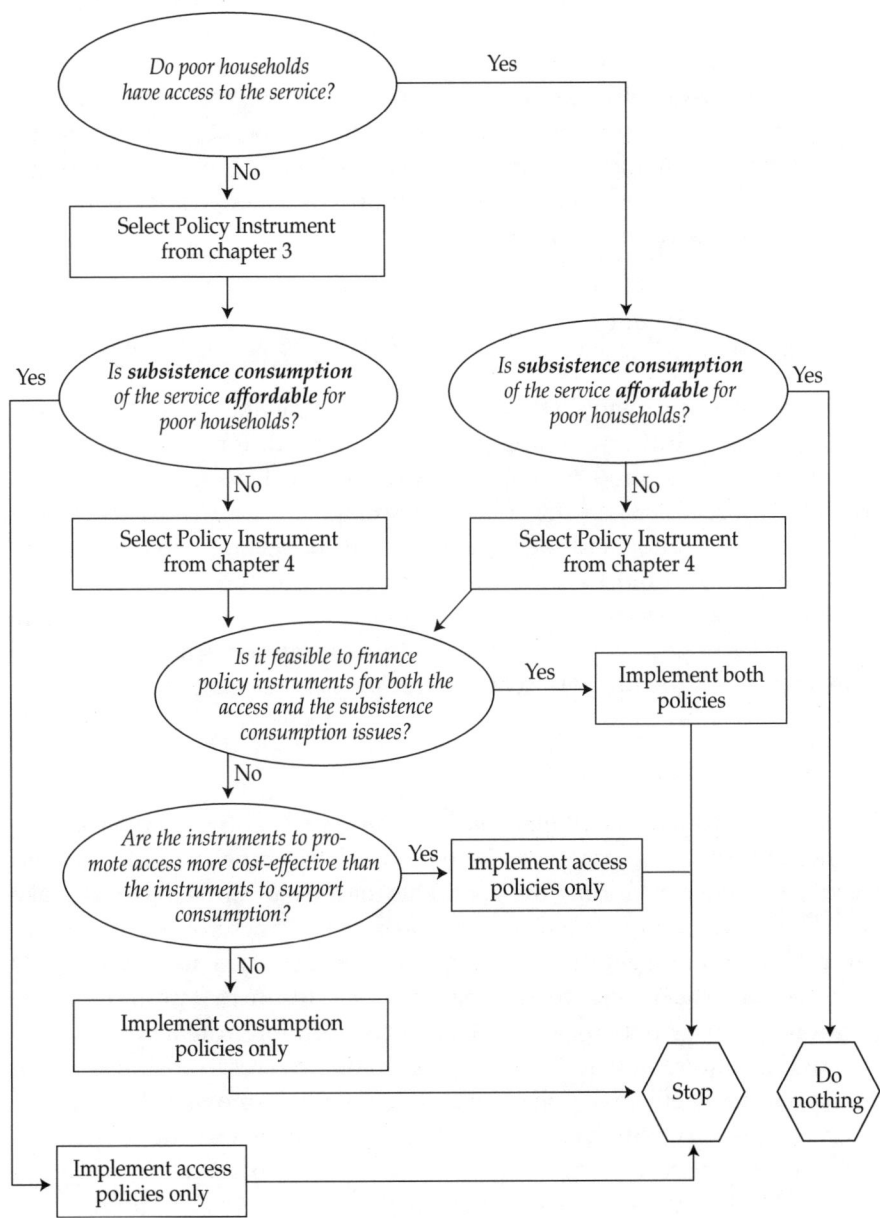

Source: Authors.

General Policy Guidelines to Protect the Poor

Recognizing that social issues should be an integral part of a successful reform and private sector participation strategy in the utility sector, what guidelines should policymakers consider when designing reforms (Estache, Gomez-Lobo, and Leipziger 2000)? One of the main lessons of this study is that the first task for most policymakers will be to generate the information needed to make an informed judgment as to the likely impact of reform on the poor. This information would then support three broad spheres of public policy discussed in this study:

- Strategy for private sector participation
- Regulatory policy
- Social policy.

These three areas should be viewed as complementary, even though the timing and institutional responsibility may be different in each case. Privatization policy and social policy actions must be considered early in the reform process to ensure that the regulatory concerns are consistent with the privatization and social goals. Any future changes in policies and social priorities should also be anticipated. Regulatory rules providing guidelines to address this kind of situation are likely to be part of the more general rules regarding renegotiation of the commitments made to the private operator at the time of private sector participation.

Strategy for Private Sector Participation

Reformers must reinforce their capacity to monitor the effectiveness of competition. The evidence reviewed here shows that competition can be good for all consumers, including the poor. This reinforces the need to undertake structural and regulatory reforms that promote competition, such as vertical and horizontal separation, elimination of exclusivity clauses in contracts and laws, and the development of a regulatory culture that promotes competition. The only potential drawback of competition from a poverty perspective is that it tends to force the elimination of cross-subsidies, which are a potentially effective policy instrument whose removal may harm the poor. However, retaining cross-subsidies is possible within the context of a competitive market as long as uniform surcharges do not discriminate between different types of customers, as with a universal access fund.

Reformers also need to pay careful attention to the investment and quality targets set at the time of privatization, especially in a concession contract as part of the definition of the service obligations imposed on the operators. If poorer households are not connected to the service, the connection targets set before privatization may have an important impact on the poor. If tariffs are sufficiently high so that serving poorer households is profitable, then a private company should extend services to these households from self-interest. However, if serving households that are more vulnerable is not profitable, investment targets may be specified in the contract. These connection targets must specify the geographic area or the type of customer who should benefit. Furthermore, the regulator will need to monitor the company to guarantee that it honors such commitments. These targets can be found throughout Latin American concessions. One way to monitor them is by including a clear specification of the universal service obligations in the scope of responsibilities of monopolies. Policymakers should also consider mandatory connection requirements in the sectoral laws. This is usually an issue in the water sector, where public health considerations make this a reasonable requirement. Connection charges, however, could be an enormous financial obstacle for poorer households unless subsidized.

Contracts with private operators should incorporate quality standards that reflect a balance between community preferences and social concerns, such as public health and safety, and these should be determined with reference to their impact on the poor. The recommendation will often be to avoid setting targets based on industrial country benchmarks that may make the service too expensive for poorer households, and to allow quality standards to be adjusted to reflect the most appropriate balance of price and quality for all parties concerned. This does not imply, however, that quality standards should not be set in the contract. Setting minimum or maximum standards—depending on the indicator and the regulatory context—is often needed to ensure that operators do not have an incentive to reduce costs and increase profits by eroding quality (under price cap regulation) or by gold-plating (under cost-plus regulation). This requires a system of sanctions that can also benefit the poor to the extent that the revenue generated from sanctions could be channeled back to poor users who may be victims of operators' abuses.

Finally, the removal of any legal obstacle that may prevent more innovative or alternative projects is an underestimated instrument in the context of privatization. Even though promoting such projects may be the task of the future regulator, avoiding at the outset any legal constraint in the contract that may limit this type of initiative is important. This is often quite complicated, as many of the poorest live at the margin of illegality, and the reform process may sometimes include policy decisions to legalize informal settlements and start their new formal existence with the formal provision of infrastructure services.

Regulatory Policy

Many actions and decisions within the traditional sphere of activities of a regulatory agency can enhance the benefits that poorer households can obtain from utility reform, building on the indications that should have already been included in the strategy for private sector participation and the design of the contracts with private operators. If the reformers support distributional concerns, laws and contracts regarding the price/quality combination should be flexible. Regulators should mirror this flexibility in their regulatory decisions, but they should also be given the mandate to take on this task with strict rules clarifying the commitments made at the time of privatization to all parties involved. This would entail permitting different combinations of these variables in different circumstances within the broad financial commitments the government makes to operators and users.

Regulators should also be reasonably open to new and innovative approaches to solve investment and operational issues related to poorer users. These include, for example, community participation in the construction and operation of networks, which may reduce their cost; the supply of communal services; and permitting small-scale private vendors or networks in certain circumstances. A regulator should not suppress such activities if they cater to an underserved market segment.

Perhaps the most effective means for a regulator to benefit lower-income users is to promote competition in services where this is possible. In addition to its impact on tariffs, competition will increase the range of available goods and services, often generating services specifically tailored to the needs of poorer households.

Finally, regulators should also allow, and even promote, the use of new and innovative tariff structures that may benefit low-income users. Ideally, services should be offered as an optional or menu choice to users. With optional or menu tariffs users can choose for themselves, and the regulator has fewer informational requirements in relation to deciding the best quality or service standards.

Social Policy

If an overriding social concern exists regarding the impact of a reform process on the poor, in principle, special countermeasures can be introduced through the welfare system. Recent experience with water concessions in Tucuman, Argentina, and Cochabamba, Bolivia, suggest that disregarding social issues altogether can be a risky strategy for reform. In both these cities, concessions had to be aborted as a result of social unrest generated by substantial tariff increases, among other factors. In many instances, the welfare system is unable to implement such countermeasures, and considering a special program for the "infrastructure poor" may make sense. Moreover, introducing distributive considerations into an infrastructure reform process, perhaps by designing a special welfare program, may be unavoidable for political reasons. The success of the privatization process may depend on such a policy, even when strict welfare considerations may not justify it.

The need for an infrastructure-specific social policy does not necessarily require that a utility regulator design, or even administer, the welfare program. On the contrary, such programs should be integrated into a government's general welfare and poverty alleviation policies, thereby maintaining coherence with complementary poverty reduction efforts and guaranteeing efficient and encompassing eligibility assessments. In the Chilean water subsidy scheme and the Colombian residential utility subsidy discussed earlier, policies in the utility industry were integrated successfully into more general welfare policies.

For special welfare programs embedded within the utility industries, the credible sustained funding of subsidies is critical. Finance can come from a variety of sources. First, governments can provide the funds from general tax revenues. This is typical for urban transport and such "negative concessions" as those awarded for many toll roads. Second, certain customers may be charged a price higher than the cost of service. This has been standard for public utilities in Latin America, and is likely to continue to be common for private utilities when governments cannot make credible commitments to finance subsidies. Third, a fund can be established to which all companies must contribute according to some proportional rule, for instance, proportional to the number of customers that each company serves or to each company's revenues. While companies will still charge a price cost markup to pay for this contribution, unlike the second case, the company is free to decide which prices and which customers to charge. In Argentina a sector-specific levy finances expansion needs in electricity distribution and transmission in the poorest provinces. In the telecommunications sector, sector-specific funds or fees have become a common mechanism for financing social obligations, with successful examples from Colombia, Guatemala, and Peru.

Which type of funding is more convenient for social policy will depend partly on the efficiency, equity, and administrative costs associated with the distortions created by the general tax system (the cost of public funds). When tax-financed subsidies are too costly to enforce and tax reform is not a realistic option, raising funds from the utility industry may be more efficient, especially if done through the fixed charge part of utility tariffs. The system selected should, however, depend on its sustainability in a competitive environment. Unlike general taxation, which is neutral for the utility industry, cross-subsidies in a competitive environment will create incentives for cream-skimming high-paying customers and ignoring low-paying ones. The third alternative avoids this last problem, as all companies will have the same proportional responsibility for funding the subsidy scheme (although this may also allow for implicit and less transparent subsidies across operational zones).

Concluding Comments

Status quo arrangements in the utility industries, such as public provision and mistargeted subsidies, are unlikely to benefit poor households. Many poor would benefit from service expansion that may be possible through privatization, which would allow them to avoid the high costs of alternative sources. Moreover, much evidence shows that many poor households are willing or able to pay for a regular and reliable service. Often, they pay much more for a deficient service. How markets are restructured, how competition is introduced and maintained, and how regulatory commitments are implemented determine whether private sector participation will benefit households. Generally, the weaker the regulatory structure, the less likely that public policy decisions will accommodate the concerns of the poor.

What is really needed is political commitment. Infrastructure reform and private sector participation do not substitute for responsible, redistributive welfare policies. However, welfare reforms are complex and tend to be slowly implemented. Policies leading to real welfare gains are needed to establish the credibility of and support for reforms that are in the interests of all in the long run. This is why, in the short run, policymakers will have to address many of the issues discussed in this study. Whether infrastructure reformers can hope to accomplish anything depends on the design and implementation strategy of these reforms. This depends on the politicians' commitment to implementation and, in particular, to fighting local interest groups that have strong interests in maintaining the status quo.

Appendix 5.1. Access to Electricity and Water by Income Decile, Selected Countries and Years

(percentage of people in each decile with access)

Country	Year	Urban				Rural			
		1st decile	3rd decile	5th decile	7th decile	1st decile	3rd decile	5th decile	7th decile
Electricity									
Brazil	1989	85.08	93.14	97.68	98.88	26.67	50.21	64.45	78.58
	1996	94.65	97.40	98.95	99.67	46.92	67.99	74.95	88.13
Chile	1992	89.10	90.44	93.98	95.20	48.47	55.29	62.89	61.62
	1998	99.52	98.97	99.27	99.71	79.03	78.05	84.13	85.24
Guatemala	1989	79.49	73.85	78.26	84.37	14.41	18.04	26.47	40.78
	1999	60.49	67.44	89.35	92.47	21.24	35.71	42.04	53.35
Honduras	1989	81.68	74.06	73.48	90.45	10.60	7.87	14.92	30.01
	1996	85.04	80.20	93.93	96.55	20.85	17.80	33.86	38.98
Mexico	1989	93.40	94.72	96.15	98.36	58.40	75.51	85.09	92.08
	1996	89.46	96.50	97.34	98.77	72.19	85.26	83.97	90.37
Venezuela	1989	99.36	99.15	99.33	99.62	83.68	81.51	82.42	87.81
	1996	99.65	99.78	98.74	99.34	93.73	96.61	100.00	98.37
Water									
Brazil	1989	52.31	64.64	82.56	91.88	11.96	27.14	44.07	63.81
	1996	73.84	81.65	91.11	96.45	20.75	43.62	57.66	76.83
Chile	1992	92.91	95.71	98.04	98.67	27.23	32.76	37.44	38.58
	1998	99.13	99.15	98.84	99.49	32.83	31.74	42.13	45.48
	1996	60.88	39.65	55.79	68.96	17.15	17.01	22.60	26.50
Guatemala	1989	65.96	66.41	67.68	73.54	25.85	32.34	36.36	42.52
	1999	51.23	78.78	83.33	88.16	46.27	44.82	40.27	43.74
Honduras	1989	87.19	80.94	86.36	81.82	83.06	91.79	87.26	81.99
	1996	83.40	84.78	85.65	89.48	70.88	79.52	81.87	85.27
Mexico	1989	64.93	82.24	88.77	94.11	41.37	52.58	62.28	70.22
	1996	76.72	86.47	90.19	93.61	44.38	62.19	63.32	69.30
Venezuela	1989	94.98	94.17	95.35	97.73	63.81	59.76	65.84	69.40
	1996	94.77	95.99	96.54	97.20	68.40	67.76	73.43	77.06

Source: Wodon and Ajwad (2000a).

References

The word "processed" describes informally reproduced works that may not be commonly available through libraries.

Abeles, M. 2000. "Evolución de Precios y Tarifas de los Servicios Públicos Privatizados." In M. Baima and A. B. Rofman, eds., *Privatizaciones e Impacto en los Sectores Populares*. World Bank-NGO Working Group, Institute for Research on the New State, Belgrano Publishers, Buenos Aires.

Ajwad, I., M. Anguizola, and Q. Wodon. 2000. "Estimating the Welfare Impact of Privatization: Electricity in Bolivia." World Bank, Washington, D.C. Processed.

Ajwad, I., and Q. Wodon. 2000. "Do Governments Maximize Access Rates to Public Services Across Areas? A Test Based on Marginal Benefit Incidence Analysis." World Bank, Washington, D.C. Processed.

Alcazar, L., M. Abdala, and M. Shirley. 1999. "The Case of the Aguas Argentinas Concession." World Bank, Development Economics Research Group, Washington, D.C. Processed.

Alexander, I., and A. Estache. 2000. "Industry Restructuring and Regulation: Building a Base for Sustainable Growth: Lessons from Latin America." *Development Southern Africa 2000* 17(3).

Alexander, M. 2000. "Privatizaciones en Argentina." In M. Baima and A. B. Rofman, eds., *Privatizaciones e Impacto en los Sectores Populares*. World Bank-NGO Working Group, Institute for Research on the New State, Belgrano Publishers, Buenos Aires.

Aschauer, D. A. 1989a. "Is Public Expenditure Productive?" *Journal of Monetary Economics* 23:177–200.

———. 1989b. "Public Investment and Productivity Growth in the Group of Seven." *Journal of Economic Perspectives* 13:17–25.

Baffes, J., and A. Shah. 1998. "Productivity of Public Spending, Sectoral Allocation Choices and Economic Growth." *Economic Development and Cultural Change* 48(2).

Benitez, D., O. Chisari, and A. Estache. 2000. "Measuring the Fiscal-Efficiency-Distribution Tradeoffs in Argentina's Utilities Privatization." World Bank Institute, Washington, D.C., and World Institute for Development Economics Research, Stockholm. Processed.

Boland, John, and Dale Whittington. 2000. "The Political Economy of Water Tariff Design in Developing Countries: Increasing Block Tariffs Versus Uniform Price with Rebate." In Ariel Dinar, ed., *The Political Economy of Water Pricing Reforms*, New York: Oxford University Press.

Carbonel, A. 2000. "Aguas del Illimani: A Case Study from La Paz-El Alto." In *Infrastructure for Development: Private Solutions and the Poor.* London: Private Provision of Infrastructure Advisory Facility, Department for International Development, and World Bank.

Chisari, O., and A. Estache. 1999. *The Needs of the Poor in Infrastructure Privatization: The Role of Universal Service Obligations: The Case of Argentina.* Discussion Paper no. 3. Buenos Aires: Argentine Business University, Economics Institute, Center for Economic Studies of Regulation.

Chisari, O., A. Estache, and C. Romero. 1999. "Winners and Losers from Privatization and Regulation of Utilities: Lessons from a General Equilibrium Model of Argentina." *World Bank Economic Review* 13(2): 357–78.

Chong, A., and J. Hentschel. 1999. "Bundling of Basic Services, Welfare and Structural Reform in Peru." World Bank, Washington, D.C. Processed.

Costello, K. W. 1988. "A Welfare Measure of a New Type of Energy Assistance Program." *Energy Journal* 9(3): 129–42.

Crampes, C., and A. Estache. 1998. "Regulatory Trade-offs in Designing Concession Contracts for Infrastructure Networks." *Utilities Policy* 7:1–13.

De la Fuente, A. 2000. "Growth and Infrastructure: A Survey." Latin America and Caribbean Region, Finance, Private Sector, and Infrastructure Department; World Bank Institute, Governance, Regulation, and Finance Department, Washington, D.C. Processed.

Eberts, R. W. 1990. "Cross-Sectional Analysis of Public Infrastructure and Regional Productivity Growth." Working Paper no. 9004. Federal Reserve Bank of Cleveland.

Erhardt, D. 2000. "Impact of Market Structure on Service Options for the Poor in Conference Volume." In *Infrastructure for Development: Private Solutions and the Poor.* London: Private Provision of Infrastructure Advisory Facility, Department for International Development, and World Bank.

Estache, A., and M. Fay. 1995. "Regional Growth in Argentina and Brazil: Determinants and Policy Options." World Bank, Washington, D.C. Processed.

Estache, A., and L. Quesada. 2001. "Infrastructure Contract Renegotiation: Some Efficiency-Equity Tradeoffs." World Bank Institute, Washington, D.C. Processed.

Estache, A., and M. Rodriguez-Pardina. 2000. "Light and Lightning at the End of the Public Tunnel." In L. Manzelli, ed., *Regulatory Policy in Latin America: Post-Privatization Realities.* Miami: North-South Center Press, University of Miami.

Estache, A., A. Gomez-Lobo, and D. Leipziger. 2000. "Utility Privatizations and the Poor's Needs in Latin America: Have We Learnt Enough to Get it Right?" In *Infrastructure for Development: Private Solutions and the Poor.* London: Private Provision of Infrastructure Advisory Facility, Department for International Development, and World Bank.

Fay, M. 2000. "Financing the Future: Infrastructure Needs in Latin America 2000–2005." Policy Research Working Paper no. 2545. World Bank, Latin America and the Caribbean Region, Finance, Private Sector, and Infrastructure Sector Unit, Washington, D.C.

Ferreira, P. C. 1996. "Investimento em infra-estrutura no Brasil: fatos estilizados e relacoes de longo prazo." *Pesquisa e Planjamento Economico* (Institute for Applied Economic Research, Rio de Janeiro) 26(2): 231–52.

Ferreira, P. C., and T. G. Malliagros. 1998. "Impactos produtivos da infraestrutura no Brasil—1950/95." *Pesquisa e Planjamento Economico* (Institute for Applied Economic Research, Rio de Janeiro) 28(2): 315–38.

Ferro, G. 1999. *Evolución del Cuadro Tarifario de Aguas Argentinas: Financiamiento de las Expansiones en Buenos Aires.* Discussion Paper no. 11. Buenos Aires: Argentine Business University, Institute of Economics, Center for Economic Studies of Regulation.

FIEL (Fundación de Investigaciones Economicas Latino-Americanas). 2000. "Subsidies in Chilean Public Utilities." World Bank Institute, Washington, D.C. Processed.

Foster, V. 2001. *Economic and Financial Evaluation of El Alto Pilot Project: Condominial Water and Sewerage Systems and Related Innovations.* Discussion Paper. Lima, Peru: Andean Region, Water and Sanitation Program.

Foster, V., and O. Irusta. 2001. "A Tale of Two Cities: Evaluating the Impact of Capitalization Reforms on Poor Households in La Paz and El Alto." World Bank, Public Private Infrastructure Advisory Facility, Washington, D.C. Processed.

Foster, V., and J. P. Tre. 2000. "Measuring the Impact of Energy Interventions on the Poor: An Illustration from Guatemala." In *Infrastructure for Development: Private Solutions and the Poor.* London: Department for International Development, Private Provision of Infrastructure Advisory Facility; and World Bank.

Foster, V., A. Gomez-Lobo, and J. Halpern. 2000. "Designing Direct Subsidies for Water and Sanitation Services. Panama: A Case Study." Policy Research Working Paper no. 2344. World Bank; Latin America and Caribbean Region; Finance, Private Sector, and Infrastructure Sector Unit, Washington, D.C.

Foster, V., J. P. Tre, and Q. Wodon. 2000a. "Energy Prices, Energy Efficiency, and Fuel Poverty." World Bank, Washington, D.C. Processed.

———. 2000b. "Energy Consumption and Income: An Inverted-U at the Household Level?" World Bank, Washington, D.C. Processed.

Galal, A., L. Jones, P. Tandon, and I. Vogelsang. 1994. *Welfare Consequences of Selling Public Enterprises: An Empirical Analysis.* Oxford, U.K.: Oxford University Press.

Garcia-Mila, T., and T. J. McGuire. 1992. "The Contribution of Publicly Provided Inputs to States' Economies." *Regional Science and Urban Economics* 22: 229–41.

Garner, H. A. 1993. "Pricing and Demand Management: A Theme Paper on Managing Water Resources to Meet Megacity Needs." World Bank, Washington, D.C.

Gomez-Lobo, A., and D. Contreras. 2000. "Subsidy Policies for the Utility Industries: A Comparison of the Chilean and Colombian Water Subsidy Schemes." University of Chile, Department of Economics, Santiago de Chile. Processed.

Guasch, J. L. 2000. "The Impact on Performance and Renegotiation of Concession Design: Lessons from an Empirical Analysis of Ten Years of Concession Experience." World Bank, Washington, D.C. Processed.

Hulten, C. R., and R. M. Schwab. 1991. "Public Capital Formation and the Growth of Regional Manufacturing Industries." *National Tax Journal* 44: 121–34.

Izaguirre, A. K. 2001. "Minimum Subsidy Concessions for Service Provision in Rural Areas: The Experience of Telecom Funds in Colombia, Guatemala, Peru, and South Africa." Presentation to the Infrastructure Forum, May 2–11. World Bank, Washington, D.C.

Izaguirre, A. K., and G. Rao. 2000. "Private Infrastructure: Private Activity Fell by 30 Percent in 1999." Private Sector Note. no. 215. World Bank, Public Policy for the Private Sector, Private Sector and Infrastructure Network, Washington, D.C.

Jadresic, A. 2000. "A Case Study on Subsidizing Rural Electrification in Chile" In *Energy Services for the World's Poor, Energy and Development Report 2000,* World Bank, Energy Sector Management Assistance Program, Washington, D.C.

Kariuki, M., and G. Acolor. 2000. "Delivery of Water Supply to Low-Income Urban Communities through the Teshie Tankers Association: A Case Study of Public-Private Initiatives in Ghana." In *Infrastructure for Development: Private Solutions and the Poor.* London: Private Provision of Infrastructure Advisory Facility, Department for International Development, and World Bank.

Kariuki, M., and B. Wandera. 2000. "Regulation of Cess Pit Emptying Services to Ensure Access for Low-Income Urban Communities: A Case Study of Public-Private Initiatives in Dar Es Salaam." In *Infrastructure for Development: Private Solutions and the Poor.* London: Private Provision of Infrastructure Advisory Facility, Department for International Development, and World Bank.

Komives, K., and P. J. Brook Cowen. 1999. *Expanding Water and Sanitation Services to Low-income Households: The Case of the La Paz-El Alto Concession,* Viewpoint Note no. 178. Washington, D.C.: World Bank, Finance, Private Sector, and Infrastructure Network.

Lanjouw, P., and M. Ravallion. 1999. "Benefit Incidence, Public Spending Reforms, and the Timing of Program Capture." *World Bank Economic Review* 13(2): 257–73.

Lerman, R., and S. Yitzhaki. 1985. "Income Inequality Effect by Income Source: A New Approach and Application to the U.S." *Review of Economics and Statistics* 67(1): 151–56.

Maddock, R., and E. Castano. 1991. "The Welfare Impact of Rising Block Pricing: Electricity in Colombia." *The Energy Journal* 12(4): 65–77.

Makdissi, P., and Q. Wodon. Forthcoming. "Consumption Dominance Curves: Testing for the Impact of Indirect Tax Reforms on Poverty." *Economics Letters.*

Melo, J. R. 2000. "Telecommunications and the Poor." In *Infrastructure for Development: Private Solutions and the Poor.* London: Private Provision of Infrastructure Advisory Facility, Department for International Development, and World Bank.

Morrison, C., and A. Schwartz. 1996. "State Infrastructure and Productive Performance." *Amercian Economic Review* 86(5): 1095–1111.

Munnell, A. H. 1990a. "Why Has Productivity Declined? Productivity and Public Investment." *New England Economic Review* (Federal Reserve Bank of Boston) (January/February): 3–22.

———. 1990b. "How Does Public Infrastructure Affect Regional Economic Performance." *New England Economic Review* (Federal Reserve Bank of Boston) (September/October): 11–32.

Nadiri, M. I., and T. P. Mamuneas. 1994. "The Effects of Public Infrastructure and R&D Capital on the Cost Structure and Performance of U.S. Manufacturing Industries." *Review of Economics and Statistics* 76: 22–37.

Navajas, F. 2000. "El impacto distributivo de los cambios en los precios relativos en la Argentina entre 1988-1998 y los efectos de las privatizaciones y la desregulacion economica." In *Fundacion de Investigaciones Economicas Latinoamericanas.* Buenos Aires: La Distribucion del Ingreso en la Argentina.

Ryan, B., and Q. Wodon. 2001. "SimSIP Goals: A Simulation Tool for Setting Development Targets." World Bank, Washington, D.C. Processed.

Serra, P. 2000. "Subsidies in Chilean Public Utilties." University of Chile, Department of Economics, Santiago de Chile. Processed.

Siaens, C., and Q. Wodon. 2000. "Impact of Access to Basic Infrastructure Services on Poverty." World Bank, Washington, D.C. Processed.

Solo, T. M. 1999a. "Small-Scale Entrepreneurs in the Urban Water, and Sanitation Market." *Environment and Urbanization* 11(1): 117–31.

———. 1999b. Aguas que yo vendo bien, aguas que yo vendo mal. In "Independent Water Entrepreneurs in Latin America: Findings in Six Cities." World Bank, Washington, D.C. Processed.

Solo, T .M., and M. Paniagua. 1999. "The Other Private Participation in Water and Sanitation: Tales of Small Independent Providers in Latin American Cities." World Bank, Washington, D.C. Processed.

Stark, O., J. E. Taylor, and S. Yitzhaki. 1986. "Remittances and Inequality." *Economic Journal* 96(383): 722–40.

Vélez, C. E. 1995. *Gasto Social y Desigualdad: Logros y Extravios*. Santafe de Bogota: Social Mission, National Planning Department.

Walker, I., F. Ordonez, P. Serrano, and J. Halpern. 2000. "Potable Water Pricing and the Poor: Evidence from Central America on the Distribution of Subsidies and on the Demand for Improved Services." Policy Working Paper no. 2468. World Bank, Washington, D.C.

Wodon, Q. 1997. "Targeting the Poor Using ROC Curves." *World Development* 25: 2083–92.

———. 2000a. "Energy Services and Programs for the Poor." World Bank, Washington, D.C. Processed.

———. 2000b. "Public Utilities and Low-Income Customers: A Marketing Approach." *International Journal of Public Sector Management* 13(3): 222–40.

———. 2000c. "Low-Income Energy Assistance and Disconnection in France." *Applied Economics Letters* 7: 775–79.

———. 2001. "Comparing Subsidies for Access and Consumption in Basic Infrastructure: A Simple Approach." World Bank, Washington, D.C. Processed.

Wodon, Q., and M. I. Ajwad. 2000a. "Marginal Benefit Incidence Analysis: An Alternative Approach." World Bank, Washington, D.C. Processed.

———. 2000b. "Infrastructure Services and the Poor: Providing Connection or Consumption Subsidies?" World Bank, Washington, D.C. Processed.

Wodon, Q., and S. Yitzhaki. 2001. "Inequality and Social Welfare." In J. Klugman, ed., *Poverty Reduction Strategies Source Book*. Washington, D.C.: World Bank.

Wodon, Q., M. I. Ajwad, and C. Siaens. 2000. "Targeting Electricity Subsidies: Lifeline or Means-Testing?" World Bank, Washington, D.C. Processed.

Wodon, Q., with contributions from R. Ayres, M. Barenstein, N. Hicks, K. Lee, W. Maloney, P. Peeters, C. Siaens, and S. Yitzhaki. 2000. *Poverty and Policy in Latin America and the Caribbean*. Technical Paper no. 467. Washington, D.C.: World Bank.

Wolff, E. N. 1996. "The Productivity Slowdown: The Culprit at Last? Follow-Up on Hutlen and Wolff." *The American Economic Review* 86: 11239–52.

World Bank. 1994. *Infrastructure for Development, World Development Report 1994*. New York: Oxford University Press.

Index

(Page numbers in italics indicate material in tables, figures, or boxes)